The Right of Necessity

Off the Fence: Morality, Politics, and Society

Series Editors:
Bob Brecher, Professor of Moral Philosophy, University of Brighton
Robin Dunford, Senior Lecturer in Globalisation and War, University of Brighton
Michael Neu, Senior Lecturer in Philosophy, Politics and Ethics, University of Brighton

Off the Fence presents short, sharply argued texts in applied moral and political philosophy, with an interdisciplinary focus. The series constitutes a source of arguments on the substantive problems that applied philosophers are concerned with: contemporary real-world issues relating to violence, human nature, justice, equality and democracy, self and society. The series demonstrates applied philosophy to be at once rigorous, relevant and accessible—philosophy-in-use.

Titles in the Series

The Right of Necessity: Moral Cosmopolitanism and Global Poverty, Alejandra Mancilla
The State and the Self: Identity and Identities, Maren Behrensen (forthcoming)
Just Liberal Violence: Sweatshops, Torture, War, Michael Neu (forthcoming)

The Right of Necessity

Moral Cosmopolitanism and Global Poverty

Alejandra Mancilla

ROWMAN &
LITTLEFIELD
———INTERNATIONAL
London • New York

Published by Rowman & Littlefield International, Ltd.
Unit A, Whitacre Mews, 26-34 Stannary Street, London SE11 4AB
www.rowmaninternational.com

Rowman & Littlefield International, Ltd. is an affiliate of Rowman & Littlefield
4501 Forbes Boulevard, Suite 200, Lanham, Maryland 20706, USA
With additional offices in Boulder, New York, Toronto (Canada), and London (UK)
www.rowman.com

Copyright © 2016 by Alejandra Mancilla

All rights reserved. No part of this book may be reproduced in any form or by any electronic or mechanical means, including information storage and retrieval systems, without written permission from the publisher, except by a reviewer who may quote passages in a review.

British Library Cataloguing in Publication Information Available
A catalogue record for this book is available from the British Library

ISBN: HB 978-1-78348-585-7
ISBN: PB 978-1-78348-586-4

Library of Congress Cataloging-in-Publication Data Available

Library of Congress Control Number: 2016946308

∞™ The paper used in this publication meets the minimum requirements of American National Standard for Information Sciences Permanence of Paper for Printed Library Materials, ANSI/NISO Z39.48-1992.

Printed in the United States of America

For T and A

'[I]t is an easy matter to talk philosophically, whilst we do not ourselves feel the hardship any farther than in speculation'.
—Samuel Pufendorf, *The Law of Nature and Nations* (1672)

Contents

Acknowledgements ... xi

1 Reviving the Right of Necessity ... 1

Part I: Historical Accounts of the Right of Necessity ... 23

2 The Right of Necessity as a Retreat to the Right of Common Use ... 25

3 The Right of Necessity and the Pull of Self-Preservation ... 45

Part II: The Right of Necessity and Global Poverty ... 63

4 Justifying the Right of Necessity ... 65

5 Content, Form and Conditions ... 81

6 The Overdemandingness Objection ... 97

7 The Right of Necessity within Moral Cosmopolitanism ... 111

Bibliography ... 117

Index ... 123

Acknowledgements

The ideas written in this book emerged, developed and crystallised between three places that I consider my academic homes: the Centre for Applied Philosophy and Public Ethics, Australian National University, Canberra; the Centre for the Study of Mind in Nature (CSMN), Faculty of Humanities, University of Oslo, Norway; and the Chilean Antarctic Institute (INACH), Punta Arenas, Chile.

For stimulating discussions, I am thankful to Ryan Bellevue, Alfonso Donoso, Christel Fricke, Bob Goodin, Nicolás Lema, and my late friend and colleague, Gerhard Øverland.

For thorough written comments and suggestions on earlier drafts of one or more of the chapters, I am thankful to Marcia Baron, Simon Birnbaum, Hans Blom, Megan Blomfield, Stephanie Collins, Jan Deckers, Göran Duus-Otterström, Andreas Føllesdal, Christel Fricke, Sarah Goff, Bob Goodin, Avery Kolers, Holly Lawford-Smith, RJ Leland, Matt Lindauer, Thomas Mautner, Grethe Netland, Kerstin Reibold, Uwe Steinhoff, Siegfried Van Duffel, and Scott Wisor.

I am especially indebted to Thomas Pogge and Tom Campbell, who supervised my PhD dissertation, from which the main claims presented in this book emerged; to Christian Barry who, as a friend and co-supervisor, was always available to help me clarify ideas; and to Gillian Brock and Samuel Fleischacker, who examined my dissertation and contributed with further comments and ideas to give it a new shape. I am also indebted to Bob Brecher and Michael Neu, editors of the Off the Fence series, for their trust all along. Meticulous, incisive and highly critical, Michael Neu was the best editor I could have hoped for. I thank him for his patience and persistence, and for helping me to untangle and clarify many points that would have otherwise been blurry.

I have also much benefited from the feedback from the audiences at the following conferences, workshops and seminars, where parts of this work were presented at different stages: Rights at the Margins workshop, University of Helsinki; Responding to Global Poverty Conference, CSMN, University of Oslo; MANCEPT workshop Global Justice: Radical Challenges, University of Manchester; political science seminar, Universidad Católica de Chile; philosophy seminar, Universidad de Concepción; political science seminar, University of Gothenburg, Sweden; political science seminar, University of Stockholm; Society for Applied Ethics Conference, University of Oxford; philosophy seminar, University of Bergen; political science and government seminar, University of Aarhus; Realizing Global Justice Conference, University of Tromsø; Centre for Applied Philosophy and Public Ethics (CAPPE) seminar, Canberra; PPPE Club, CSMN, University of Oslo; Australasian Association of Philosophy Conference, University of Otago; Research School of Social Sciences seminar, Australian National University; and philosophy seminar, Charles Sturt University, Wagga-Wagga.

In writing the book, I have used bits and pieces from the following two articles, and I am thankful to the publishers for allowing me to do so: 'What the Old Right of Necessity Can Do for the Contemporary Global Poor', in *Journal of Applied Philosophy*, DOI:10.1111/japp.12170; and 'Samuel Pufendorf and the Right of Necessity', in *Aporia* 3 (2012): 47–64.

This work was partly supported by the Research Council of Norway through its Centres of Excellence funding scheme, project number 179566/V20. I also appreciate the financial support offered by the Society for Applied Philosophy to organise the workshop A Place for the Old Right of Necessity in the Contemporary Debate on Global Poverty, CSMN, University of Oslo, and that of the Consejo de Ciencia y Tecnología (CONICYT), Chile, for giving me a four-year scholarship to pursue my doctoral studies at the Australian National University, where it all began.

Finally, I thank Rita for her ongoing support; Tomás for his company and for our long conversations on the topic, sustained through the years, along Lake Burley Griffin, Sognsvann and the Straits of Magellan; and Alma for her light.

ONE
Reviving the Right of Necessity

As I write these lines, in 2015, 836 million people live with less than 1.25 dollars a day. Seven hundred ninety-five million people (that is, one in nine people on earth) do not have enough food to lead a healthy, active life. Seven hundred fifty million people lack access to clean water, and 16,000 children under the age of five die each day due to preventable causes like diarrhoea, malaria and pneumonia.[1] At the same time, wealth inequality worldwide has been on the rise since the 2008 economic crisis. Currently, it is estimated that the richest 1 percent of adult wealth holders now own half of all household wealth, reaching levels not seen for almost a century.[2]

The first four statistics are enough to give a flavour of the scale of world poverty today and the high toll it takes on human lives. The last one, related to global wealth inequality, points to the huge gap between the realities of those in need and those who have resources in abundance. All together, they constitute the raw material from which a growing number of moral and political theorists have posed the question of what moral duties, if any, affluent countries and individuals owe to the poor.

Because of their influence and pervasiveness in this debate, in what follows I focus my analysis on a particular strand of analytic political theorists—namely, moral cosmopolitans. Broadly construed, moral cosmopolitanism aims at diminishing human suffering and at respecting and promoting human rights and justice on a global scale, starting from three assumptions: that individual human beings are the ultimate unit of moral concern (*individuality*); that this status attaches to every human being equally (*universality*), and that this status is to be acknowledged by everyone else (*generality*).[3] Without fear of oversimplifying, I suggest that the answers of moral cosmopolitans to the above question could be classified in two main groups, depending on which kind of duties are emphasised.[4]

On the one hand, what I hereafter call *justice cosmopolitans* answer the question from a global justice perspective. As Thomas Pogge, one of its most prominent exponents, explains, the focus of this view is 'the causal and moral analysis of the global institutional order against the background of its feasible and reachable alternatives'.[5] To design and redesign international and supranational institutions so that they do not cause insecure access to the objects of basic human rights in a foreseeable and avoidable way is the goal of this position, inspired by Rawls's conception of justice as the first virtue of social institutions. The implication is that those who are better-off under the current global structure, and especially those who have greater influence and bargaining power, have above all negative duties not to support or participate in the creation of global institutional arrangements that uphold injustice, and not to contribute to, or profit from, them.[6]

In Pogge's view, the *coercive* social institutions that constitute the global order are directly responsible for the unfulfiled human rights of the poor, while all individuals who participate in it are indirect contributors, and should stop being so. It is thus assumed that there is a causal, though indirect, link between the plight of the needy and the actions of all those involved in the imposition of such institutions—where *involvement* is understood in a broad way.[7]

On the other hand, *assistance cosmopolitans,* as I tag them from now on, emphasise assistance as the main moral duty that the global affluent owe to the global poor. Where justice cosmopolitans trace causal connections between the actions of the wealthy and the plight of the needy in order to ground the duties of the former, assistance cosmopolitans simply look at the jaw-dropping economic and social inequalities in the world today and conclude that those who are in a position to aid are failing to do enough to diminish the total amount of suffering. For Peter Singer, the most prominent assistance cosmopolitan, there are no excuses to go on failing on this duty, especially given at what little cost the better-off could actually make a positive difference. He formulates his argument for an obligation to assist thus: 'If it is in our power to prevent something bad from happening, without sacrificing anything nearly as important, it is wrong not to do so'.[8] Considering, as he claims, that never before has the world seen so many rich people ('there are about a billion living at a level of affluence never previously known except in the courts of kings and nobles'[9]), saving the lives of the more than two billion living in abject poverty is presented as a relatively cheap moral task, and makes it all the more appalling not to do something about it.[10]

Depending on what they think is the minimum morally required from those in a position to help (in terms of money, time and effort), assistance cosmopolitans range from those who demand that agents change their current ways of living dramatically, to those who argue for a more moderate duty to help the poor that is to be balanced against other important moral considerations—for example, personal projects and relationships.[11] In general, assistance cosmopolitans propose that this positive duty to aid should be exercised mainly through governmental and nongovernmental agencies, while some seek the institutionalisation of aid at the supra-national level, via some sort of global taxation.[12]

This is an extremely succinct presentation of the positions of justice and assistance cosmopolitans. It should be enough, however, to restate the point made at the beginning: despite the different justifications offered, both sides focus on what the well-off are *doing* that has a detrimental impact on the lives of those in need, or on what the well-off are *failing to do* that would have a beneficial impact on them, and, thence, on the *duties* derived. Furthermore, even when the suggestion is that the world's rich are violating the human *rights* of billions, the conclusion is that *we*, the lucky ones (and, not surprisingly, moral and political theorists always fall on this side of the division), ought to fix the problem by upholding *our* duties of justice or assistance, or both.

In this book, I focus on the other side of the coin—that is, I focus on what having a human right to subsistence actually and practically means for their holders, and on what actions it allows them to undertake when it remains unfulfiled. That is, my main interest is on what the needy may be morally permitted to do by themselves and for themselves to fulfil or satisfy their basic right to subsistence, given the unjust structures that keep them in a state of deprivation, or given the insufficient assistance they get from those who could easily offer it, or both. This question has been mostly overlooked in the debate so far conducted, where the materially privileged seem also to be the morally anointed to address the plight of the worse-off.[13] Instead of characterising the needy as passive recipients of whatever the wealthy decide to do on their behalf, I thus take them to be agents whose role in a cosmopolitan morality has been insufficiently explored. This analysis is therefore thought of as a necessary complement to the analyses so far advanced.

To look at the issue from this standpoint becomes all the more pressing if one looks at some straightforward figures. Applying Pogge's own estimations, 18 million people die prematurely every year from easily preventable poverty-related causes, representing one-third of all human deaths.[14] If this really constitutes the largest (if not the gravest) human rights violation in the history of humankind, as Pogge contends,[15] and if those who are perpetrating this massive violation persist doing so, it is timely to ask what those whose very self-preservation is endangered may do for themselves in such a scenario. Regarding global assistance, a quick look at the amounts donated to the poor by rich citizens and countries through NGOs and governmental agencies in the last years and at the actual efforts to put in place international and supra-national mechanisms such as a global tax, indicate that the majority of those who ought to aid are failing to do so, or not doing enough, even if this comes at a minimal cost to themselves.[16] In this context, to ask what those in need may do about their plight in the meantime does not seem out of place.

In a nutshell, the answer offered is the following. Starting from the assumption that there is a basic right to subsistence, my claim is that, given three individually necessary and jointly sufficient conditions, a chronically deprived agent has a *right of necessity* to take, use and/or occupy the material resources required to guarantee her self-preservation, or the means necessary to obtain the latter—where these material resources may include a space to be and to inhabit—even if this means encroaching upon the property of third parties. The conditions are that the need in question is basic, that the person in need does not violate other equally important moral interests to exercise her right, and that it is a last resort.[17] In a hypothetical society where the basic right to subsistence of all individuals is secured under normal circumstances, the exercise of this right would be truly exceptional and mostly confined to one-off emergencies. On the contrary, in the world as it is, where millions suffer from chronic deprivation and where it is at least doubtful that they will exit that state any time soon, the exercise of the right of necessity could turn out to be a much more common occurrence.

The idea of a permissible right of the poor to take someone else's property to get out of their plight is not new, but inspired by medieval and early modern accounts which expand the traditional, narrow understanding of *necessity*. Since ancient times, *necessity* was thought to 'break through the ties of all laws' (Seneca was the one to make that claim[18]), and it was used to justify all sorts of otherwise wrongful acts if done in order to survive. For example, throwing the cargo overboard to prevent a ship from sinking, or feeding on human flesh when on the brink of famine. The originality of medieval and early modern theorists resides in that they enlarge the umbrella of necessity to include not only one-off emergencies that were mostly naturally caused but also cases of chronic deprivation that seemed to result from structural inadequacies of the social and institutional context.[19]

Regarding the form of the right, I suggest that it is a *liberty* in the sense that Judith Jarvis Thomson gives to this term when dissecting Wesley Newcomb Hohfeld's famous typology of rights.[20] A *liberty*, in this sense, is a *privilege* compounded with a *claim of non-interference* against others. In Hohfeldian terminology, if A has a *privilege* to ϕ (where ϕ is an action), A is free to ϕ—that is, she has no duty not to ϕ. But having a privilege does not entail that A has a *claim* against other parties to ϕ. In the case in point, if the needy agent merely had a privilege to take, use and/or occupy the resources needed, this would mean that, given certain conditions, she would be morally free to do so. This, however, would not correlate with any duties of the owner of x or any other person for that matter. What is more, the agent's privilege to take, use and/or occupy the resources needed might well collide with the privilege of the owner to defend his property against intruders, needy or not, or with the privilege of any other third parties to impede the agent's actions.[21] This is why it is insufficient to understand the right of necessity as a privilege alone, and why it must be supplemented by a relational claim of non-interference against others, including the owner of the targeted resources. The right of necessity, as I propose to understand it, thus leaves the agent a space of freedom to act which others are duty-bound to respect.

The focus of this book, then, is on the right of necessity as a concrete manifestation of the right to subsistence. Talk of duties is not absent, however, but forms a key part of the discussion. This does not render invalid my initial critique of the cosmopolitan debate on global poverty and its overemphasis on duties talk. Insofar as rights and duties are correlative (that is, insofar as a right is conceptualised as a claim against someone to do or not to do something), rights talk and duties talk go necessarily hand in hand. My point is rather to underline that human rights in general—and the basic right to subsistence in particular—are also action-guiding, contrary to Onora O'Neill's contention that 'those who claim still see themselves within an overall framework of recipience', and that 'they still demand that others act rather than they do so themselves'.[22] Instead of assuming that those bearing the duties are the only ones entitled to take steps towards the universal fulfilment of basic subsistence rights, it is reminded here that basic rights as claims may be actively realised by the individual holders in the last instance, even if this implies breaking the law. In these situations, those bearing the correlative duties fulfil them by not interfering: immediately, for example, by letting the former take what they require without resistance, and by not turning them in to the police, and mediately, by not guarding their property in such a way that is inaccessible for those who may need it.

As I expound in chapter 5, a key distinction to be made is between mediate and immediate duties correlated to the right of necessity and final duties aimed at the universal realisation of the basic right to subsistence. As just mentioned, the former are specific duties not to interfere with the needy agent on the spot, and also general duties not to make one's resources unavailable to those who may claim necessity to them. The latter, meanwhile, include positive duties *to protect* people from falling into deprivation, and *to aid* them directly if needed, and above all negative duties *not to deprive* people of their means available to satisfy their basic needs.[23] Using the right of necessity as a normative compass, these final duties might be ultimately reconceptualised as duties not to create and/or uphold conditions under which people may permissibly claim their right of necessity while being at the same time incapacitated from exercising it, or, positively stated, duties to create conditions under which the exercise of the right of necessity by the chronically deprived eventually disappears.

The acknowledgement that allocating these final duties and complying with them is the crucial step towards eradicating global poverty should not distract us, then, from the fact that those undergoing deprivation may do something about their own situation *now*, even if their actions turn out to be disruptive for the current state of affairs—actually, a bit of disruption might be exactly what is needed to set agents in motion to comply with their final duties. Moreover, that theoretically empowering the needy to exercise their right will make no difference in practice to many of them (because the resources needed are inaccessible) should not speak against the importance of upholding this right, but rather against an economic system that impedes those lacking the most basic material resources from obtaining them by both legal and illegal means.

These statements constitute the core thesis of this book. They are relatively simple, and the complexity will come, above all, from explicating the main concepts, applying them to contemporary scenarios, and addressing the main objections to the principle and its applications.

THE RIGHT OF NECESSITY AND PROPERTY RIGHTS

In his much quoted essay, 'A Right to Do Wrong', Jeremy Waldron characterises what seems to be a standard belief in contemporary moral theory—namely, that individuals have the right to make certain choices within a certain range where they are not to be interfered with, even if these choices are morally wrong. One of these rights, according to Waldron, is to do with our property what we wish, without external interference, even though we could use it for much worthier ends—more specifically, charitable ends. In his view, the decision of someone who has just won the lottery to spend all his money on champagne and horse races instead of giving it to people who really need it is a sort of wrongdoing that should be tolerated by others, for the sake of protecting the individual's freedom of choice, of paramount importance in liberal moral theory.[24]

But, as Waldron himself acknowledges, rights to do wrong are not without boundaries, and their moral legitimacy obviously hinges upon the rights of others. An important aim of this project is to show that, in the specific case of being able to do with one's property as one wishes, one such boundary is set precisely by the right to subsistence of others, a vital human interest the moral importance of which outweighs other non-vital human interests. Furthermore, my claim is that the right of necessity—understood as a concrete expression of the right to subsistence—is not an external but an internal limitation to any reasonable system of property rights. In this sense, the purpose of delineating the right to do wrong and the purpose of delineating the right of necessity are congenial:

they both seek to carve a protected space of free choice for the individual; a space which is deemed as essential for both his own well-being and that of society as a whole. In another sense, however, they differ: in the case of the former, the main concern is to protect the autonomous sphere of those who already own enough material resources, so that they may do as they wish with them or, at least, so that they may not have them subjected to the whims and will of others. This protection is backed up by the laws, the police and the social conventions. In the case of the latter, on the contrary, the main concern is to protect the autonomous sphere of those who are lacking even the most basic resources, so that they may get them even if this means helping themselves to someone else's belongings. This protection (unless in exceptional one-off cases) is not backed up but hindered by the laws, the police, and the social conventions.

A claim of this sort provokes immediate suspicion in a context where respect for property, no matter how petty and superfluous, is almost taken as sacred by the law and by common morality. My aim is to show, however, that if one understands the respect and fulfilment of the basic right to subsistence as providing a justificatory foundation for any reasonable property system, this much follows: to wit, that those whose basic right to subsistence goes unmet should not be required to abide by laws that keep them in that state, but may actively take measures conducive to its fulfilment by other means, even if these imply violating those very laws.

Although I defend a minimalistic version of the right to subsistence and, therefore, of the right of necessity, this defence has nonetheless major normative ramifications for what needy people in the world may do, and for what many other people in the world have a duty to let the needy do. Furthermore, such a defence, despite being minimalistic, makes it morally incumbent to rearrange global property arrangements in a way that does not leave millions of people in a position where they may legitimately invoke their right of necessity. This is not to say that a minimalistic version of the right of necessity such as the one I offer is the only defensible one; rather, it is to say that, despite the explicit minimalism of the argument put forward in this book, no reasonable defender of property arrangements can avoid its far-reaching implications.

SCOPE AND LIMITS

To set the limits of this project more clearly, in this section I mark its differences with three other approaches that seem closely related. These are subsistence wars and poor-led political movements, the possibility of *forced assistance*, and the legal rendering of the right of necessity.

The Right of Necessity vis-à-vis Subsistence Wars and Poor-Led Movements

Among justice cosmopolitans, there are a few authors who have defended the view that needy states or organised groups may wage war against affluent states, if the latter are violating their basic human rights. If the rights violated are subsistence rights, then the war waged by the needy against the affluent is a *subsistence war*. As Cécile Fabre summarises:

> [C]ontroversially ... cosmopolitan justice sometimes permits the very deprived to wage war against those who treat them unjustly. Subsistence rights ... are important enough to warrant defending by force provided that wrongdoers who meet the conditions for liability to attack can be identified.[25]

For Fabre, this might involve killing culpable civilians who contribute in a relevant way to the plight of the poor, inflicting non-lethal harm upon those who contribute in more indirect ways to their plight, and even killing the latter unintentionally, but with foresight, in the course of war.[26]

With war cosmopolitans, I share the assumption that the right to subsistence is of such paramount moral importance that it may be defended by the right-holders themselves if no one else is able to guarantee it. There are three features of their account, however, that I find problematic, and that set my account apart from theirs.

First, my analysis focuses on what *individuals* may do to alleviate their need. The right of necessity is eminently an individual right, held and exercised by individual people (this does not preclude, of course, that needy individuals may then get organised and act together). War cosmopolitans, on the contrary, start from deprived *states* or *collectives* as the relevant agents for an obvious reason: it is hardly imaginable to think of deprived individuals waging war against those who wrongfully keep them in such a state. But this brings an obvious complication: for the sake of argument, war cosmopolitans tend to divide countries into rich and poor, and to ignore the socioeconomic differences within them. Kasper Lippert-Rasmussen, for example, makes the conditional claim that, if what Pogge says regarding the millions of deaths caused by the affluents' failure to comply with their duties of justice globally is true, then the poor may engage in a just and maybe even permissible war against the former. Among the 'simplifying assumptions' needed for this hypothetical exercise to work is that 'the world divides into two groups of states: poor states populated with poor people only and rich states populated with rich people only'![27] Fabre, meanwhile, admits that it is methodologically inadequate to regard whole countries, as opposed to individuals, as affluent or deprived. Regardless, 'for the sake of stylistic convenience', she does use the labels of *rich* and *poor* to refer to states as well as to individuals.[28] Even if a mere stylistic decision, this is problematic, insofar as it unduly oversimplifies the reality of global poverty, where the well-off and the deprived coexist side by side, with poverty and sharp socioeconomic inequalities turning into a threat in developed countries, and millionaires and billionaires flourishing in developing ones.[29] Moreover, it also ignores interconnectedness in the way, for instance, in which the elites from the centre and the periphery strike bargains to the detriment of their respective populations.

Second, war cosmopolitans claim that a necessary condition for waging a just subsistence war is that those against whom the war is waged are *liable*—that is, they have violated the subsistence rights of those waging the war in such a way as to make this extreme form of self-defence permissible. For Fabre, a just cause of war may be that those now liable wrongfully took away property that was required by others to satisfy their basic needs, or failed to revert property to the common stock where that property was also instrumental for others to satisfy their basic needs, or held policies that contributed to the severe deprivation of others (like protectionist policies and patent laws), or refused to help others who were suffering because of having their basic needs unmet. Thus, the causal connection between the actions of the wrongdoers and the suffering of those waging war has to be clear and certain, especially given the serious implications at stake.[30] Instead, throughout this book I ask what the needy may do not only against those who directly contributed to their plight or blatantly failed to meet their duty to fulfil their basic subsistence rights but also against *almost* anyone else. I say *almost* because, as was said above, one of the conditions for this right to hold is that its exercise does not violate other equally important moral interests of others. In practice, this means that the right of necessity does not permit a needy person to take what she needs from someone in a similar plight, or to make a claim that would jeopardise the basic liberties of others—that is, unless her claim of necessity is compounded with a claim of justice (I explore this idea further in chapter 5). That the needy may stake a claim upon *almost* anyone else is based on the idea that we live in a sufficiently interconnected and interdependent global economic order for it to create certain minimal claims against, and certain minimal duties towards, each other. What I have in mind is something along the lines of Iris Marion Young's *social connection model of responsibility*, in which people bear responsibility towards others insofar as they participate in institutional processes that create and maintain structural injustices.[31]

Third and finally, war cosmopolitans make the moral permissibility of subsistence wars hinge upon controversial requirements such as proportionality and non-futility—that is, the costs of waging the war should not be disproportionate to the wrongs that trigger going to war, and there should be a reasonable expectation of success.[32] But waging a war requires at least a good organisational apparatus, money for weapons and an army of well-fed and well-trained soldiers, and not even then is there a guarantee that the attempts to wage war will not be futile. This makes it highly unlikely that those in need will ever meet these requirements, thus turning subsistence wars in more of a theoretical exercise than a practical possibility. As Fabre herself admits, ultimately echoing the generalised attitude that depicts the deprived as helpless beings, '[P]ut starkly, what hope do the scores of desperately poor individuals throughout the world—many of them children and women with burdensome family responsibilities—have to arm themselves and act in defence of their rights? None whatsoever'.[33]

On the contrary, the idea that individuals may exercise their right of necessity to satisfy their basic needs is no mere theoretical exercise, but a real possibility. Let me mention two examples. During the 1950s and through the 1960s and 1970s, the urban homeless in Santiago, Chile, developed a method whereby individual families settled overnight in empty patches of land that were publicly or privately owned, but unoccupied, to form together what came to be known as *poblaciones callampas* (or *mushroom settlements*, given their sudden appearance).[34] These actions were always carried out in a pacific way, even though the *callamperos* did resist if threatened with eviction and invoked their right of necessity to a place to be when no other alternatives were available to them. Today, in a context where prices of basic consumption items soar, while wages and welfare benefits shrink in many countries, many have turned to shoplifting or to buying knockoff groceries as a means of getting their food and basic medical provisions for them and their families. Although I cannot offer here a case-by-case analysis to judge whether all these actions have been carried out because of necessity, news reports reveal that agents intuitively appeal to the last resort condition and that, as a result, many times those whose property is being taken or those who are supposed to enforce the law against them, condone, rather than condemn, the former's actions.[35]

Still, it might be thought that there are those among justice cosmopolitans who have already focused on the role of the poor as agents in a cosmopolitan morality and, more specifically, on their role towards the fulfilment of their basic right to subsistence. Along these lines, Monique Deveaux has recently argued that poor-led movements in the global South have played and are playing a key part in the success of strategies of poverty reduction and development, opposing views that consider only or mainly the well-off as the agents of global justice. More critically, Roberto Gargarella has questioned whether those whose basic human rights are being violated have a duty to obey the very laws that keep them in a state of deprivation, or whether they may legitimately resist them, as well as the authorities that contribute to their imposition. Relatedly, Simon Caney has conceptualised the 'Right of Resistance against Global Injustice' as what any agent is entitled to do to change the underlying social, economic and political practices and structures in a more just direction.[36]

I share the main tenets from which advocates of poor-led movements depart, but there are at least two differences between their approaches and mine. The first is that, like war cosmopolitans, their analyses are focused on the actions of *organised collectives* rather than *individuals*. The second is that these actions are above all intended as *political* actions designed to change the current state of affairs for the benefit of the poor in general, with a long-term view. For Deveaux, these collectives are communities of poor people and pro-poor solidarity networks and movements, contributing with their knowledge, deeds and decision making to the building of policies that both reduce extreme poverty and empower them as social and political agents. For Gargarella, the relevant agents are organised citizens who, deprived and oppressed, defy through active or passive resistance illegitimate laws and the authorities that support them. For Caney (who does not restrict this right only to the poor, but to 'all rights-holders who are able to do so'), there is the further requirement that agents 'should act in ways that realize the values that underpin the vision we should be striving towards'.[37] In practice, this means that the agent's actions are constrained by requirements of fairness, and aim at making the world a better place.

On the other hand, the right of necessity, as will be repeatedly stressed, is the expression of an individual moral prerogative primarily aimed at securing one's self-preservation when the latter is at stake. It is thus not conceived, at least not in the first instance, as a political right aimed at political change directed at achieving social justice. As the book unfolds, however, it should become clear that the exercise of the right of necessity might trigger social and political movements that demand structural changes for the benefit of the needy as a whole. Defending the principle of necessity is thus not antithetical to the positions above presented, but should be seen as providing an argument, at a very foundational level, as to why these movements should be let to be, and as to why one should listen to them and engage with them insofar as one is concerned with the eradication of global poverty.

The Right of Necessity vis-à-vis Forced Assistance

A subset of assistance cosmopolitans advocate *forced assistance*—namely, the idea that it is morally permissible to act against the will of those who can do something at little cost to themselves and to the great benefit of the needy but nonetheless fail to do so.[38] Peter Unger, for example, endorses what he calls *simple appropriation*: to steal or use what is another's, even if it is of considerable monetary value, without their consent and without compensation for the loss imposed, the only condition being that the appropriation be 'far less than any truly serious loss'.

When required to lessen the serious suffering of 'innocent enough people', this seems like an acceptable moral path, or so Unger contends.[39] Similarly, Gerhard Øverland endorses the moral permissibility of forced assistance by focusing on individual cases of rescue. And while he admits that the question of the duties of the global wealthy towards the global poor is not exactly analogous and demands a separate investigation, he hints at the possibility that it could be answered by the same principle: 'Given that thousands of people are dying from poverty-related causes each day and we live in affluent societies with ample means to help a substantial part of this world's needy population, the permissibility of using force against ourselves to assist the global poor cannot be easily dismissed'.[40] Furthermore, Øverland openly admits that '[i]t seems plausible to assume that a person could be justified in taking some of my property to fend off starvation ... Many people seem to accept that no one has a right not to give food to a starving person on one's doorstep'. If this is the case, extrapolating this to the global level would result in our permission 'to take certain measures to ensure that "donation" takes place, for instance, by diverting money illegally from an affluent person to famine relief'.[41]

There are two things worth underlining from Unger's and Øverland's accounts. One is the recognition that the duty of assistance in some instances is of such moral importance that it should not be left entirely to the bearer's discretion whether to comply with it. The other is that, by touching upon the common intuition that to avoid starvation may justify taking someone else's property, the possibility of justifying a right of necessity therefrom is paved.

Having said this, three features of these accounts set them apart from the one here presented. One is that, even though they hint in passing at the possibility that the deprived may act by themselves to get out of their plight, they ultimately focus on what third parties may do for them on their behalf. Consequently, advocates of forced assistance perpetuate the view that the needy are generally passive recipients who require the aid of others in order to exercise their claims—where these others tend to be characterised as well-off individuals ready to act in Robin Hood style. By contrast, while I acknowledge that transitivity is a property of the right of necessity (so that this right may be exercised by others on behalf of the holder), my main aim is not to coax others into becoming self-appointed representatives of the worse-off. It is easy to fall prey to romanticised paternalism, but this ultimately does a disservice to the cause of the needy, by reinforcing their characterisation as patients rather than agents; on the contrary, it should be the needy themselves who decide who they wish to have their claims enacted by.[42]

Second, given the stark opposition that the idea of simple appropriation would generate given the prevailing moral norms, Unger acknowledges that such a recommendation should be omitted altogether if the objective is to motivate moral conduct in general. Øverland also underlines the importance of considering the likely cost that a conduct like *forced donation* would have, all things considered. And he concludes that, because to force someone to do something can easily imply resorting to disproportionate means, this path of action may frequently be morally impermissible.[43] This means that, while espousing quite daring moral precepts in principle, Unger and Øverland end up with quite tepid moral recommendations in practice. Here, on the contrary, my aim is to show that accepting the existence of a human right to subsistence in principle leads to quite radical implications in practice; implications that we should be willing to accept if we don't want to turn it into an empty, rhetorical *manifesto right*.[44] To be sure, considerations of cost and proportionality must come into the picture when analysing the possibility of exercising the right of necessity case by case, but these considerations should not count as deterrents against upholding the principle; quite the opposite, they should be an enticement to think of ways in which to turn the exercise of the right of necessity into a truly exceptional occurrence.

Third, like other assistance cosmopolitans, advocates of forced assistance downplay the importance of global economic structures and processes in the generation of global poverty. By focusing almost exclusively on the duties of those who are *capable* of giving aid, they neglect the analysis of duties arising from our interdependence and interconnectedness in one global economic structure, where some flourish while others wane. On the contrary, a key feature of the argument to come is that partaking in one global economic order generates a final duty not to create and/or uphold conditions under which people fall into a situation such that they may claim necessity while being at the same time prevented from exercising it. An analysis of the moral prerogatives of individuals in dire need that ignored the context where this need arises would be incomplete at best and misleading at worst.

The Moral vis-à-vis the Legal Conception of Necessity

Some might wonder what is novel about the project that I am here proposing, considering that necessity has always had a place among the criminal law defences of both common law and civil law systems.[45] In them, necessity standardly refers to cases of lesser evil or choice of evils— that is, when 'a man has his choice of two evils before him, and, being under a necessity of choosing one, he chooses the least pernicious of the two'.[46] A classic example is that of the unlucky hiker who is caught in a mountain storm and must break into someone else's hut in order to save himself from dying in the cold.[47]

There is a long debate in the legal literature as to whether cases like the above should be seen as providing a justification or an excuse-based defence, as to whether the threat triggering the harm done must be natural, and as to whether defences of necessity should be restricted to situations where the act was done for the sake of furthering a greater social good or interest (for example, when a crop field has to be burnt down in order to stop a raging forest fire that threatens a whole town), rather than for the benefit of a sole individual acting under unbearable pressure or coercion.[48] For the purposes of the discussion, however, what is important to highlight is that no legal system considers cases of chronic material deprivation as providing either a justification or an excuse for taking, using and/or occupying the property of third parties. On the contrary, as succinctly stated in *Lord Simon of Glaisdale in DPP v. Lynch*, 'It is certainly not the law that what would otherwise be the theft of a loaf ceases to be criminal if the taker is starving'.[49]

By restricting its scope in such a way, thus, the law denies such a right to those who remain hungry and homeless due to the action or inaction of human third parties, individual or institutional, and limits itself almost exclusively to one-off situations of need rather than to continued states of deprivation.[50] Instead, as said above, I propose to revive a conception of the right of necessity that emerged during medieval times in response to the question of what may permissibly be done by individuals who are in a chronic state of deprivation which is attributable to the way in which human institutions are framed, rather than to one-off events of bad cosmic (or meteorological) luck. That is, I propose to revive a conception of the right of necessity that is distinct regarding both the type of threat (human-caused and permanent, rather than natural or human-caused and one-off) and the kind of need at stake (ongoing versus exceptional). Unless I explicitly say so, in what follows I thereby leave aside discussion of stranded hikers and focus on the right of necessity in this particular sense.

ASSUMPTIONS

There are four normative and two factual assumptions that underlie this project. The normative assumptions are moral cosmopolitanism, the existence of a basic human right to subsistence, the acceptance of the institution of property as a salutary social arrangement, and the belief that any reasonable system of property must have the satisfaction of everyone's basic needs built into it as an internal limitation. The factual assumptions are the existence of *favourable conditions*, and the belief that the overwhelming majority of humans today partake in a common global economic structure (within which property arrangements play a prominent role). My claim is that, if one shares these assumptions, on reading this book and accepting its main arguments one will be led to think about cosmopolitan rights and duties maybe (drastically) differently than one was used to. A remapping of the normative landscape of moral cosmopolitanism is therefore where this project seeks to lead.

As mentioned above, despite the diversity of philosophical positions that fall under its umbrella, moral cosmopolitanism can be distinguished by its endorsement of individualism, universality and generality as its three main tenets.[51] Even if it is in a minimal sense, being a moral cosmopolitan means believing, in other words, that there is such a thing as a *global moral society* of which all human beings are part, and in which we all bear certain duties to, and hold certain rights against, each other.

The second assumption (as explained in more detail in chapter 4) is that all individuals hold certain basic rights. These are rights upon which the fulfilment of all other rights depend, and the right to subsistence is one of them.[52] Combined with moral cosmopolitanism, this leads to the claim that, as members of one global moral society, we should recognise these basic rights, including the right to subsistence, on all others.

Third, I also assume that property rights in whatever shape they come (private, collective, communal) are a salutary social arrangement, insofar as they further some essential aims of the individual. Among these aims are, most importantly, security of possession and the tranquillity that our basic needs are going to be met. Because of these beneficial effects, we respect property rules and we give up certain freedoms and powers that we had or would have had (depending on whether we pick a historical or hypothetical version) in a state of nature scenario. In other words, it is not part of this project to criticise the institution of property as such, and it is not part of this project to put into question some commonly cited reasons as to why establishing property arrangements in a community of otherwise free individuals serves several other important functions — among them, to ensure that the things put under individual control are going to be better cared for than if they remained under no one's power; to bring about more orderly and peaceful mutual relations, by making clear what belongs to whom; to promote human industry and ingenuity, and to enhance aggregate economic performance; to make it possible for people to make plans and projects with the reasonable expectation that the basic institutional framework will be kept, and so on and so forth.

The fourth assumption is that, for the above reasons and especially insofar as they further the aims of guaranteeing a certain level of security and the satisfaction of basic needs, it is reasonable for individuals to accept and respect property arrangements. Inversely, if property arrangements do not give these minimal guarantees, then accepting and respecting them would be unreasonable. Put differently, if someone ends up destitute under a property scheme whose basic rules are justified precisely in terms of securing and providing at least a minimal threshold of material resources for everyone, then that person may not be expected to abide by those rules. Some might complain that these two assumptions about property arrangements ignore the complex processes underlying and shaping them. For example, it might be the case that the very same processes giving rise to property take away the minimal guarantees that I claim should be built into any reasonable property regime, and that this is not an aberration, but an embedded feature. Accordingly, the analysis ought to take into account these complexities. This worry, however, is misplaced: my strategy is to show that *if* one is a staunch defender of property rights as producing all sorts of beneficial effects, *then* one must also accept that the right to subsistence (and, therefore, the right of necessity as a concrete expression of the latter) must be built into them as an internal limitation. What I am questioning, then, is not the viability of the institution of property, but rather the idea that being a property rights advocate runs at odds with defending the right of necessity for the chronically deprived.

Regarding the factual assumptions, first, I assume that certain minimally favourable material and technological conditions hold at the global level, that make it not utopian but feasible to have everyone's basic right to subsistence satisfied under normal circumstances. In times of generalised famine or environmental catastrophe, presumably, other principles would apply.

Second, I assume that there is such a thing as a *basic global economic structure* of which most human beings are currently part. Two key features of this global structure that matter for this project are the more or less universal acceptance of institutionalised property and production regimes worldwide (regimes which are increasingly interconnected and interdependent) and the de facto existence of a world made of states into which we are all born, states that not only regulate the principles for the distribution of goods and services but also constrain our movement as individuals and, therefore, our life prospects and projects. That this structure exists and that we all partake in it and in its processes is especially relevant when it comes to the justification of the right of necessity as a claim with correlated duties that is not only domestically but also globally binding.

THE COMING CHAPTERS

The conception of the right of necessity here presented is not new; it has a long philosophical pedigree that goes back to medieval Christian canonists and theologians, the best known of whom is Thomas Aquinas.[53] The idea persists well into the eighteenth century, especially among modern natural law theorists such as Hugo Grotius, Samuel Pufendorf, John Locke, Emer De Vattel, and Francis Hutcheson.[54] In part I, I review what I consider to be the most developed accounts of this principle, while pointing to their main strengths and weaknesses. Bringing in this historical analysis is important insofar as the authors under examination offer some key insights regarding the main topics that keep resurfacing throughout the book—to wit, the foundation of basic rights, the primary social function of property arrangements and the internal limits of the latter; the form, content and conditions that the right of necessity should have; and the visionary idea that, on striving towards a just society, one of the aims should be to turn the right of necessity into a truly exceptional prerogative.

In chapter 2, I go back to the origins of the right of necessity in the thought of some Christian canon lawyers and theologians from the end of the twelfth century onward. I focus particularly on Aquinas, who shares with his contemporaries the view that the right of necessity is the revival of the original, pre-institutional right of common use of the earth's resources. I then present Hugo Grotius's account as a secularised version of the former. Because Grotius (at least explicitly) seems to understand this right as a mere *privilege* rather than as a *claim* (i.e., as a bare freedom to act that creates no correlative duties on third parties not to interfere with the needy's actions), I argue that this raises intractable problems, and contradicts some of the conditions that he himself sets for the exercise of this right. By contrast, I suggest in chapter 3 that Pufendorf's understanding of this right as creating an enforceable duty to aid on those who have the means to fulfil it is more satisfactory, as is his visionary claim that a minimal requirement for any coercive institutional framework (paradigmatically, property schemes) is to ensure that no one falls under the necessity threshold. Rather than appealing to a retreat to the state of common use, Pufendorf bases the right of necessity on the basic human pull for self-preservation.

After examining these historical accounts, in part II I spell out the place that the right of necessity should have in the contemporary debate on global poverty and moral cosmopolitanism. In chapter 4 I offer five different arguments for the existence of a basic right to subsistence, and explain why the right of necessity should be understood as a concrete manifestation of it. In a hypothetical society where the universal fulfilment of the basic right to subsistence is guaranteed under normal circumstances, the exercise of the right of necessity would be confined to exceptional circumstances like the hiker-in-the-storm kind of scenario. In a society where individuals suffer chronic deprivation, on the contrary, the exercise of the right of necessity should be accepted as the least one should grant to those who have no other means to subsist. I then suggest how these normative findings should lead moral cosmopolitans to remap the normative landscape of rights and duties in the global poverty debate.

In chapter 5 I spell out the content, form and conditions of the right of necessity. Regarding its content, I take it to be whatever material resources one needs to subsist, or to the means required to obtain them. Regarding its form, I propose to understand the right of necessity as a *liberty*: a *privilege* coupled with a *claim of non-interference* against third parties, which generates both immediate and mediate duties of non-interference, as well as final duties on others. I then spell out three individually necessary and jointly sufficient conditions for the exercise of the right of necessity. These are that the need in question is basic, the exercise of the right does not violate other equally important moral interests, and it is a last resort.

In chapter 6, I address the objection that the right of necessity might turn out to be an overly demanding moral principle epistemically, psychologically and theoretically. I propose a two-tiered recommendation that ought to be followed inasmuch as possible by the claimants, in order to reduce potentially unfair outcomes, and address the objection that the exercise of the right of necessity might leave unaffected those directly responsible for the needy's plight.

In chapter 7, I address the worry that theoretically empowering the needy is of little use in practice if those who may permissibly claim their right are practically unable to do it. I conclude by flagging three issues that merit further exploration if the right of necessity is incorporated within cosmopolitan morality—namely, the reconceptualisation of a large sub-group of economic and environmental migrants as necessity claimants; the implications of the idea that the right of necessity may be exercised by others on one's behalf; and the question of whether using the right of necessity as a normative compass with which to evaluate the legitimacy of our current global economic order should lead us to conclude that, rather than minor adjustments, what the latter needs is a radical change if the goal is to fulfil the basic right to subsistence of all those partaking in it.

NOTES

1. See, respectively, United Nations, Millennium Development Goals Report 2015 (2015), 4, http://www.un.org/millenniumgoals/2015_MDG_Report/pdf/MDG%202015%20rev%20%28July%201%29.pdf; Water Organization, 'Millions Lack Safe Water', http://water.org/water-crisis/water-facts/water/; United Nations, Millennium Development Goals Report 2015, 8–9; and UNICEF, http://www.data.unicef.org/child-mortality-under-five.html, all accessed October 15, 2015.

2. Credit Suisse Research Institute, *Global Wealth Report 2015*, accessed October 15, 2015, http://publications.credit-suisse.com/tasks/render/file/index.cfm?fileid=C26E3824-E868-56E0-CCA04D4BB9B9ADD5, 12. *Wealth* is defined in this study as 'the value of financial assets plus real assets (principally housing) owned by households, less their debts'. Moreover, the study frames its results in terms of the global *adult* population, estimated to be around 4.8 billion in 2015.

3. Thomas Pogge, *World Poverty and Human Rights: Cosmopolitan Responsibilities and Reforms*, 2nd ed. (Malden, MA: Polity Press, 2008), 175.

4. To build a thorough taxonomy of the positions in the global justice/global assistance debate would constitute an altogether different project. Within each group, there are neither shared definitions of *justice* and *assistance* nor agreement on the demandingness of the moral constraints that each duty imposes. Moreover, although both

groups agree that the objects of these duties are individual human beings, they do not always coincide on who the duty-bearers should be (individuals, groups, countries, international or supra-national institutions?). They also assign different weight to pragmatic considerations and to moral motivation: for example, should we balance the importance of these duties depending on how motivated people are to comply with them, or should we stick to what we consider to be the right principles, regardless of people's pull to comply? Last, but not least, justice and assistance cosmopolitanism cover a whole range of different normative frameworks, from rights theory to act utilitarianism.

5. Thomas Pogge, *Politics as Usual* (Cambridge: Polity Press, 2010), 24.

6. Pogge, *World Poverty and Human Rights*, 203.

7. Pogge, *World Poverty and Human Rights*, 178. Some more ambitious justice cosmopolitans have suggested that focusing on these institutional negative duties is insufficient, and that achieving global justice requires not only the performance of negative duties not to harm, directly or indirectly, but also positive duties to aid. See, for example, Pablo Gilabert, 'The Duty to Eradicate Global Poverty: Positive or Negative?', *Ethical Theory and Moral Practice* 7, 5 (2004). What both views agree on, nonetheless, is that the main moral task demanded to end the plight of the global poor is to build a just global basic structure, and that undertaking this moral task is required by all those who participate in the current structure—with all the more reason the better positioned they are to bring about effective change.

8. Peter Singer, *The Life You Can Save* (Melbourne: Text Publishing, 2009), 15. Over the years, Singer has offered different formulations of the same principle that imply different levels of demands on agents. This is the most recent one, and by far the most moderate.

9. Singer, *The Life You Can Save*, 9.

10. For a similar defence of *effective altruism*, see William MacAskill, *Doing Good Better: How Effective Altruism Can Help You Make a Difference* (London: Gotham, 2015).

11. The most demanding versions of assistance cosmopolitanism are those espoused by Peter Singer in his seminal article, 'Famine, Affluence, and Morality', *Philosophy and Public Affairs* 1, 3 (1972): 229–43, and by Peter Unger, *Living High and Letting Die* (New York: Oxford University Press, 1996). More moderate versions are found in Liam B. Murphy, 'The Demands of Beneficence', *Philosophy and Public Affairs* 22, 4 (1993); Brad Hooker, *Ideal Code, Real World: A Rule-Consequentialist Theory of Morality* (Oxford and New York: Clarendon Press, 2000); Garrett Cullity, *The Moral Demands of Affluence* (New York: Clarendon Press, 2004); and Richard W. Miller, 'Beneficence, Duty and Distance', *Philosophy and Public Affairs* 32, 4 (2004).

12. See, for example, Tom Campbell's proposal for a Global Humanitarian Levy: Tom Campbell, 'Poverty as a Violation of Human Rights: Inhumanity or Injustice?' in *Freedom from Poverty as a Human Right*, ed. Thomas Pogge (New York: Oxford University Press, 2007), 67.

13. I present some exceptions later in this chapter.

14. Pogge, *World Poverty and Human Rights*, 2.

15. In contrast with other massive human rights violations, such as the Nazi extermination of the Jews, or the premeditated starvation of millions of Russian peasants under Stalin's rule, the current violation is not the *gravest*, because the *violators* do not intend those deaths directly, but rather cause them through negligence, self-deceit, and so on. Pogge, *Politics as Usual*, 51.

16. Singer estimates that, over the last five decades, aid from rich to poor countries has been merely about 30 cents from every 100 USD earned, and this does not even take into account the fact that a high percentage of that aid is based on political or defence considerations, rather than humanitarian ones. Singer, *The Life You Can Save*, 114.

17. While endorsing the language of human rights, the main claims of this book work equally well for those who use the language of interests or preferences instead. Thus, one could say that the basic *interest* in subsistence or the strong *preference* that

humans show for subsistence is of such key moral importance that it justifies leaving to the individual the moral prerogative to defend it when it is endangered and when there are no other means to guarantee it—even if this implies breaking the law.

18. Quoted in Hugo Grotius, *The Law of War and Peace (DJB)*, trans. F. W. Kelsey (Washington, DC: Carnegie Institution, 1913), II.II.6, 193.

19. To be clear, this is not something that they explicitly said, but rather my own interpretation of their writings.

20. Judith Jarvis Thomson, *The Realm of Rights* (Cambridge, MA: Harvard University Press, 1990), 54.

21. Wesley Newcomb Hohfeld, 'Some Fundamental Legal Conceptions as Applied in Judicial Reasoning', *Yale Law Journal* 23, 1 (1913): 36.

22. Onora O'Neill, 'Rights, Obligations and Needs', in *Necessary Goods*, ed. Gillian Brock (Lanham, MD: Rowman & Littlefield, 1998), 97.

23. The typology of duties of *avoidance, protection* and *aid* is from Henry Shue, *Basic Rights: Subsistence, Affluence, and U.S. Foreign Policy*, 2nd ed. (Princeton, NJ: Princeton University Press, 1996): 51ff.

24. Jeremy Waldron, 'A Right to Do Wrong', *Ethics* 92, 1 (1981): 21.

25. Cécile Fabre, *Cosmopolitan War* (Oxford: Oxford University Press, 2012), 100–101. A similar argument is given by David Luban, 'Just War and Human Rights', *Philosophy & Public Affairs* 9, 2 (1980).

26. Fabre, *Cosmopolitan War*, 126.

27. Kasper Lippert-Rasmussen, 'Global Injustice and Redistributive Wars', *Law, Ethics and Philosophy* 1, 1 (2013): 67. To be fair, Lippert-Rasmussen is aware of this over-simplification, but his aim is not so much to propose the conditions for actual subsistence wars as to carry Pogge's premises to a seemingly unpalatable conclusion. See also Thomas Pogge, 'Poverty and Violence', *Law Ethics and Philosophy* 1, 1 (2013).

28. Fabre, *Cosmopolitan War*, 101.

29. Regarding the first phenomenon, in the last three decades wage gaps widened and household inequality increased in a large majority of Organisation for Economic Co-operation and Development (OECD) countries: *Divided We Stand: Why Inequality Keeps Rising* (2011), http://www.keepeek.com/Digital-Asset-Management/oecd/social-issues-migration-health/the-causes-of-growing-inequalities-in-oecd-countries_978926 4119536-en. In Germany, to quote one case, income poverty has been increasing gradually for the last three decades: Olaf Groh-Samberg, 'Increasing Persistent Poverty in Germany', German Institute for Economic Research (DIW), vol. 3, 2007. In the United States, to quote another, the number of Americans living below the official poverty line in 2011 reached its peak in over half a century according to the Census Bureau, with 46.2 million people: Sabrina Tavernise, 'Soaring Poverty Casts Spotlight on Lost Decade', *New York Times*, September 13, 2011, http://www.nytimes.com/2011/09/14/us/14census.html?_r=0. At the same time, almost half of the world's millionaires live today in the United States: Credit Suisse Research Institute, *Global Wealth Report 2015*, 46. Regarding the second phenomenon: China, India and Brazil (three developing countries with swooping social and economic inequalities) ranked second, fourth and seventh among the ten countries with the highest number of billionaires in the *Forbes 2015 Survey of the Richest of the Richest*: China counted 213, followed by India with 90, and Brazil with 50: *Forbes Magazine*, 'The World's Billionaires', http://www.forbes.com/billionaires/list/, all accessed October 15, 2015.

30. Fabre, *Cosmopolitan War*, 126.

31. Iris Marion Young, 'Responsibility and Global Justice: A Social Connection Model', *Social Philosophy and Policy* 23, 1 (2006), 115ff.

32. For a critique of the non-futility condition, see Uwe Steinhoff, *On the Ethics of War and Terrorism* (Oxford: Oxford University Press, 2007).

33. Fabre, *Cosmopolitan War*, 117.

34. Mario Garcés, *Tomando su sitio: El movimiento de pobladores de Santiago 1957–1970* (Santiago de Chile: LOM Ediciones, 2002), 29–34.

35. See, for example, Patrick Butler, 'Food Poverty: "I Was Brought Up Not to Steal: But That's How Bad It's Got"', *Guardian,* June 24, 2013, http://www.theguardian.com/society/patrick-butler-cuts-blog/2013/jun/24/food-poverty-growth-in-shoplifting-groceries; 'Kansas Officer Sent to Arrest Shoplifting Mom Pays for Her Groceries Instead', *Fox News,* July 12, 2015, http://www.foxnews.com/us/2015/07/12/instead-arresting-shoplifting-mom-kansas-cop-buys-items/; and Lauren Davidson, 'Shoplifting in Russia Is Soaring as the Economy Crumbles', *Telegraph,* July 23, 2015, http://www.telegraph.co.uk/finance/economics/11759336/Shoplifting-in-Russia-is-soaring-as-the-economy-crumbles.html, all accessed October 15, 2015.

36. See Monique Deveaux, 'The Global Poor as Agents of Justice', *Journal of Moral Philosophy* 12 (2015): 127; Roberto Gargarella, 'The Right of Resistance in Situations of Severe Deprivation', in *Freedom from Poverty as a Human Right,* ed. Thomas Pogge (New York: Oxford University Press, 2007), 359–60; and Simon Caney, 'Responding to Global Injustice: On the Right of Resistance', *Social Philosophy and Policy* 32, 1 (2015).

37. Caney, 'Responding to Global Injustice', 62 and 67.

38. I borrow this term from Gerhard Øverland, 'Forced Assistance', *Law and Philosophy* 28, 2 (2009).

39. Unger, *Living High,* 63 and 82.

40. Øverland, 'Forced Assistance', 231–32.

41. Gerhard Øverland, 'The Right to Do Wrong', *Law and Philosophy* 26, 4 (2007): 393 and 394.

42. In short, I do not rule out that the needy may resort to well-off agents (activists or hacktivists, for example) if the latter have a better chance to exercise their rights on their behalf. However, this is not the focus of inquiry of this book.

43. Øverland, 'Right to Do Wrong', 393.

44. The term *manifesto right* was coined by Joel Feinberg: 'A person is always "in a position" to make a claim, even when there is no one in the corresponding position to do anything about it. Such claims, based on need alone, are "permanent possibilities of rights," the natural seed from which rights grow. Manifesto writers are easily forgiven for speaking of them as if they were already actual rights, for this is but a powerful way of expressing the conviction that they ought to be recognized by states as potential rights and consequently as determinants of present aspirations and guides to present policies'. Joel Feinberg, *Social Philosophy* (Englewood Cliffs, NJ: Prentice-Hall, 1973), 67.

45. See, for example, *Model Penal Code Annotated* (Proposed Official Draft 1962), Criminal Law Web, accessed January 7, 2016, http://www.law-lib.utoronto.ca/bclc/crimweb/web1/mpc/mpc.html#fn1, §3.02.

46. William Blackstone, quoted in Joshua Dressler, 'Exegesis of the Law of Duress: Justifying the Excuse and Searching for Its Proper Limits', *Southern California Law Review* 62 (1988): 1347.

47. See Joel Feinberg, 'Voluntary Euthanasia and the Inalienable Right to Life', *Philosophy & Public Affairs* 7, 2 (1978): 102.

48. On the first point, see George P. Fletcher, 'The Individualization of Excusing Conditions', in *Justification and Excuse in the Criminal Law,* ed. Michael Louis Corrado (New York: Garland Publishing, 1994), 57 and 87. On the second point, see Joshua Dressler, who distinguishes *necessity* from *duress* depending on the origin of the threat: 'when a lightning storm forces D to trespass on V's land in order to seek safety, [a plea of necessity may be invoked]. When the threat is human in origin—e.g., an armed terrorist threatens to kill D unless he drives on V's land—only a plea of duress potentially may be invoked': Dressler, 'Exegesis', 1348. On the third point, see Paul H. Robinson, 'Criminal Law Defenses: A Systematic Analysis', *Columbia Law Review* 82, 2 (1982): 213.

49. Quoted in Jeremy Waldron, 'Why Indigence Is Not a Justification', in *From Social Justice to Criminal Justice,* ed. Hugh Heffernan and John Kleinig (Oxford: Oxford University Press, 2000), 99. See also *London Borough of Southwark v. Williams,* where the English Court of Appeal denied that extreme hunger could excuse a theft or that

homelessness could excuse a trespass. The reason, said Lord Denning, was that 'if hunger were once allowed to be an excuse for stealing, it would open a door through which all kinds of disorder and lawlessness would pass'. Denning, in turn, relied on the seventeenth-century Lord Chief Justice of England, Matthew Hale, who claimed that 'if necessity could justify theft, men's properties would be under a strange insecurity, being laid open to other men's necessities, whereof no man can possibly judge, but the party himself': Alan Brudner, 'A Theory of Necessity', *Oxford Journal of Legal Studies* 7, 3 (1987): 340.

50. A detailed *explanation* of why the law functions thus is offered in Waldron, 'Why Indigence Is Not a Justification'.

51. Pogge, *World Poverty and Human Rights*, 175.

52. Here I follow Shue, *Basic Rights*, 19.

53. St. Thomas Aquinas, *Summa Theologica*, trans. Fathers of the English Dominican Province, 2nd and rev. ed. (1920) II-II, Question 32, Article 6, and Question 66, Article 7, accessed July 17, 2015, http://www.newadvent.org/summa/.

54. See Grotius, *DJB* II.II.6, 193–94; Samuel Pufendorf, *Of the Law of Nature and Nations*, trans. Basil Kennet, fourth edition, 8 vols. (London: Printed for J. Walthoe, 1729), II.VI, 202–12; John Locke, *Two Treatises of Government*, ed. Peter Laslett (Cambridge: Cambridge University Press, 1988), I.§42, 170; Emer De Vattel, *The Law of Nations*, ed. Béla Kaposy and Richard Whatmore (Indianapolis: Liberty Fund, 2008), II.I and II.IX; and Francis Hutcheson, *A System of Moral Philosophy in Three Books*, ed. William Leechman, 2 vols. (Glasgow: Printed by R. and A. Foulis, 1755), II.XVII, 117–40.

Part I

Historical Accounts of the Right of Necessity

TWO
The Right of Necessity as a Retreat to the Right of Common Use

Although the question of what duties the global wealthy owe to the global poor might sound like a novel topic in moral and political philosophy, what is really novel about it is its scope. In Western thought, the idea that the wealthy had stringent moral duties towards the needy, and that these had a legitimate claim against the former was already present in late medieval Europe, when a group of Christian canonists and theologians started questioning whether it was really the case that it was better to starve than to sin (namely, by stealing to survive), when those who had a duty to aid had failed to do so. Their conclusion was, rather, that a person in need may rightfully take someone else's property with or without the consent of the owner in order to get out of her plight, and that by so doing he was not committing a sin by *stealing* but barely *using* what was common by natural law, independently of what human laws had established.

It is this framework that the early modern natural law thinkers inherited and developed. Well into the eighteenth century, the right of necessity was still a standard assumption of moral and political philosophers in this tradition (a more contested point was whether it was matched by a correlated duty and, if so, of what kind). Different formulations can be found in the writings of Thomas Hobbes, Hugo Grotius, Francisco de Vitoria, John Locke, Samuel Pufendorf, Gershom Carmichael, Jean Barbeyrac, Francis Hutcheson and Emer De Vattel, among others.[1]

In this chapter, I present the main medieval arguments to justify this right, founded on the idea of humanity's right of common use of the earth and its resources. I focus particularly on Thomas Aquinas's account and underline its main features. I then go on to present Hugo Grotius's version of the right of necessity as in continuity with the medieval tradition, and point to its main strengths and weaknesses. I give a rather lengthy treatment of these accounts (and also of Pufendorf's, in chapter 3), because it is on them that I base my own account in the coming chapters. If the right of necessity is to have a place in the contemporary philosophical discussion on global poverty, I suggest that its form, content and justification will be largely in line with those given by these authors. While acknowledging the challenge of transposing concepts from one historical context to another, I think that translatability and commensurability are possible (*pace* MacIntyre), so long as one is aware of the different contexts.[2]

One more clarification is in place before proceeding, which concerns the choice of authors under examination. Why focus on Aquinas, Grotius and Pufendorf rather than, say, other equally important theorists like Hobbes, Locke and Hutcheson? Is there anything special about them that the others are lacking, or is this just a random selection? Without purporting to carry out an exhaustive survey of the right of necessity in the history of philosophy, I focus on these authors insofar as I take them to present the more developed and detailed accounts of this right, and to share the main normative and factual assumptions that guide my own inquiry. As mentioned in chapter 1, these assumptions are moral cosmopolitanism and the recognition of a basic right to subsistence; an understanding of property rights as a beneficial social arrangement that is internally limited by a regard to the basic right to subsistence of all society's members; and the factual assumption that certain favourable conditions hold, so that the exercise of the right of necessity is materially possible—in other words, the context is such that there are enough resources available to satisfy at least the basic needs of everyone, and their distribution is feasible.[3]

Having said this, it will be clearer why I choose to leave out Hobbes, who starts his analysis from a purely self-centred view of human nature. As a proto-utilitarian, meanwhile, Hutcheson turns the right of necessity on its head, by conceptualising it as a necessary exception to preserve the well-being of society over that of individuals when they are at odds. He thus claims that 'all the rights of individuals, and all the special rules of life should be postponed to the universal interest of all ... Of all the social laws that is the most sacred, which prefers the general interest and safety to that of individuals or small parties'.[4] In fact, even though he devotes a whole chapter of his *System of Moral Philosophy* to 'The Extraordinary Rights Arising from Some Singular Necessity', there is only one passage where Hutcheson allows for the possibility of individuals claiming this right, and this only insofar as it promotes rather than hinders the short and long-term general utility: '[T]he public interest is really promoted, when an innocent man saves himself from some great evil by some small damage done to another'.[5]

Meanwhile, Locke's account of the right of necessity (which he never calls by that name, but the *right to the charity of others*) is brief and focused exclusively on the duties that it gives rise to. Its justification, moreover, does not appear in the context of his treatment of property rights, but in his *First Treatise of Government*, directed at refuting Robert Filmer's arguments for the right to absolute monarchy of Adam's direct descendants. Along Aquinas's lines, Locke gives there a theological argument whereby God has left none of his sons in such a position that others may starve him if they please. When someone is under pressing need, thus, he has a right to the surplus of others, 'so that it cannot justly be denied him'.[6] As opposed to Aquinas, however, Locke never implies that this right to the charity of others is an active right. On the contrary, the poor are not supposed to take action, expecting that action be taken for them by the well-off.[7] In this point, his views are remarkably close to those of justice and assistance cosmopolitans who concentrate on the duties of the haves, while confining the have-nots to the position of forbearing recipients.

A MEDIEVAL PRELUDE

Until the end of the twelfth century in Europe, in a time where the threat of famine and abject poverty were ever present, the teachings of the Church Fathers and the sermons inspired on them and delivered to the Christian congregations focused above all on the duty of the wealthy to be charitable. 'Feed him that is dying of hunger; if thou hast not fed him, thou hast slain him', famously commanded Saint Ambrose of Milan: 'It is the hungry man's bread that you detain; the naked man's clothes that you store away; the poor man's ransom and freedom that it is in the money which you bury in the ground'.[8] The inflamed rhetoric regarding what the rich ought to do for the needy, however, was not matched by any equivalent advice to the needy to claim the bread, clothes, ransom, or freedom that was supposed to belong to them. On the contrary, doing so without the consent of the owners was regarded as theft and condemned as a sin.

But this changed at the end of that century, generally regarded as a time of spiritual and intellectual renaissance and renewal.[9] It was then when canon lawyers and theologians started questioning the standard patristic teachings or, rather, tried to show that the right of the needy to take matters into their own hands logically followed from them. The idea was basically this: because God gave the earth to all human beings, in the original state everyone was free to take whatever they needed to subsist. This was understood as a state of *negative community*, where the earth was not owned by each and every person according to some equal share, but everyone could get what was required for their immediate consumption.[10] At a later period, human laws and institutions (private property stellar among them) were created to preserve that original equality in the best possible way, while advancing the well-being of everyone. If it ever was the case, though, that in civil society someone came to be in a state of extreme need, she may demand assistance. If this help was denied, she may take what is needed or have someone do it on her behalf. Thus, a wife could offer alms even without the consent of her stingy husband, and so could a monk, without the consent of his uncharitable abbot. An administrator could also use the goods entrusted to him to relieve someone from dire need, and even usurers could choose to help the needy before making restitution of their ill-gotten money. As for the ruler, prince or bishop, it was generally agreed that in times of famine they could compel the wealthy to give alms or require merchants to lower food prices.[11] The human-made law of property could thence never trump the natural law of common use; on the contrary, it had to consider it as prior, so that whenever they clashed the latter was to take precedence.

The canonist Huguccio, around 1190, is arguably the first to articulate this idea:

> When it is said that by natural *ius* all things are common ... this is the meaning. By natural *ius*, that is, in accordance with the judgment of reason, all things are common, that is they are to be shared with the poor in times of need. For reason naturally leads us to suppose that we should keep only what is necessary and distribute what is left to the needy.[12]

From then on and for a couple of centuries, this was generally the accepted view, although there was quite a fair bit of disagreement regarding the fine print. One point of heated debate was how to define the *extreme* necessity required to authorise the poor to take action. Did the person have to be on the brink of imminent death, or was the threat of imminent death enough to let them act? The latter was the more popular view, but there were also some more radical ones. The churchmen Angelo de Clavasio and Sylvester Prieras, for example, proposed that it was enough justification for the poor to take the surplus of the rich if the rich had failed to aid them in the first place, even if the former were not yet in extreme need. A different point of disagreement was whether, having helped themselves, the poor had any duties of restitution. For the Dominicans, there was no such duty because they were merely claiming their due; for other religious orders, by contrast, some sort of compensation or at least a sign of gratitude were expected.[13]

The best-known medieval version of the right of necessity is that of Thomas Aquinas (1225–1274), whose views in this matter were opposed to those of Aristotle and Augustine, considered the common standard for centuries.

Both Aristotle and Augustine classified every kind of theft as morally condemnable, even if the purpose was to help someone in dire need. Aristotle classified theft among the type of actions that are always bad, so that 'it is not possible, then, ever to be right with regard to them; one must always be wrong'.[14] Augustine, meanwhile, reasoned that, because it was unlawful to steal in order to give alms to one's neighbour, it was also unlawful to steal in order to fulfil one's own need. Aquinas's reply is that 'it is not theft, [p]roperly speaking, to take secretly and use another's property in a case of extreme need: because that which he takes for the support of his life becomes his own property by reason of that need'.[15] He supports his claim thus: by natural law, there are certain things (paradigmatically, food) that are meant for our sustenance. With human law these *lower things* become divided and appropriated, but this does not eliminate the fact that we still need them in order to stay alive. For this reason, human law cannot cancel out natural law in cases where the only way for a person to survive is by using someone else's property.

The default procedure suggested by Aquinas to ensure that no one falls in dire need is to give to the poor all things owned in superabundance, as 'each one is entrusted with the stewardship of his own things, so that out of them he may come to the aid of those who are in need'.[16] When the necessity is clear and urgent, however, taking someone else's property is allowed, openly or secretly, directly by the needy or indirectly by someone on their behalf. This moral prerogative is open to every human being, Christian or not, insofar as we all share the faculty of reason, which gives us a special status in nature and entitle us to the use and possession of God's creation. In this framework, private property (as those before him had repeatedly stressed) is a supplement to natural law and fulfils above all a social function, so that there is nothing objectionable with putting it into brackets if following the rules to the letter hinders that fulfilment.[17] Moreover, given that keeping oneself alive was a duty towards God, the right of necessity was not simply an option but also an obligation.[18]

Although it has been contested whether Aquinas supports a right of necessity for those in a permanently deprived situation (he says, after all, that the need has to be *urgent*[19]), a host of other theologians and canonists from the twelfth and thirteenth century enlarge the understanding of the right of necessity to cover this kind of case. Thus, in his *Defense of the Poor* (*Apologia pauperum*), the Italian theologian Bonaventure (1221–1274) claims that '[t]he first form of common possessions is that which flows from the right of the necessity of nature ... through which anything required for the sustainment of natural life becomes the share of the man who is in extreme need of it, even though it may have been appropriated by someone else'.[20] The English canonist Alanus remarks that 'the poor man did not steal because what he took was really his own *iure naturali* — which could mean either "by natural right" or "by natural law"'. Laurentius Hispanus (1180–1248) writes that when the poor man took what he needed, it was 'as if he used his own right and his own thing', and the Italian canonist Hostiensis (1200–1271) states that 'one who suffers the need of hunger seems to use his right (*ius suum*) rather than to plan a theft'.[21]

The quotes above serve to highlight seven important features of the medieval account of the right of necessity, which persist (with some variation) in the accounts of Grotius and Pufendorf. First, it is a universal right possessed by all of us solely by virtue of who we are—that is, rational creatures in permanent need of material things to stay alive, and who hold a symmetrical claim to the use of the earth and its resources for our benefit. Second, what triggers the right of necessity is need pure and simple, regardless of its genesis, and regardless of it being part of a one-off emergency or a more sustained state of material deprivation. Third, the right of necessity may be exercised even against the will of the owner. Fourth, this may be done either openly or secretly. Fifth, it must be exercised only as a last resort. Sixth, it is a transitive right that others may exercise on our behalf.[22] Seventh and finally, it is not pictured as conflicting with property rights, but rather as uncovering the purpose for which the latter were originally instituted—namely, to guarantee everyone's basic sustenance.[23]

But, how was the right of necessity exercised in the actual medieval world? It turns out that, despite being part of the 'Christian common sense',[24] it hardly ever entered the realm of common or civil law, and remained almost entirely restricted to the domain of morality, theology and canon law. This restriction is not surprising, considering that those in power must have foreseen its dangerous political implications and so preferred to rule it out altogether. It is worth mentioning, however, two notable exceptions. One of them regards the Swedish Provincial Laws from the twelfth century, where in cases of necessity taking a maximum of five turnips per person was allowed, with no restitution required.[25] The other case regards the English law which, while not explicitly endorsing the exercise of this right, excepted from punishment those who took from others a smaller amount than what was considered basic for subsistence. Thus, according to the law book *Britton*, a compilation of English laws that appeared in French, under the reign of King Edward I (1239–1307), 'infants under age and poor persons (and idiots and madmen) who out of hunger burgled for victuals of less value than twelve pence, could not be convicted of this crime'. At the time, twelve pence was enough to buy an ox: '[T]he reason for the limit to be fixed at 12*d*. was that this amounted to eight days' wages ... and as a man going without sustenance for eight days might be expected to die on the ninth, the 12*d*. has regard to the destruction of life, for which offense a man is rightfully put to death'.[26]

That the right of necessity was generally rejected as a principle of common and civil law created an unsatisfactory situation for the potential claimants: not much was gained by having moral and even divine authorisation to take what they needed if, when they got caught, the human laws could send them to the gallows. As Brian Tierney notes, canon lawyers put forward the following solution. After satisfying one's own needs, it was assumed that everyone in society had the obligation to help sustain the lives of others. This was not an obligation of civil law, but of moral and canon law. Correspondingly, those who failed to comply with this obligation did not end up in civil courts under charges of crime, but could well end up in the bishop's office under charges of sin — not a minor issue in a world where the church had as much (if not more) power than civil authorities, and where the fears of eternal damnation were taken quite seriously. This happened when the needy brought their claims to the ecclesiastical authority in a procedure known as *evangelical denunciation*, the sanctions of which went from penances to excommunication. To do this, the claimants did not pay court fees or legal counsel, as the first were waived and priests were allowed to prosecute their cases, playing the role of *necessity experts*.[27] In this way, the right of necessity was prevented from becoming a toothless rhetorical device, but it was also far from being a standard institutionalised procedure, as some commentators have recently suggested.[28]

HUGO GROTIUS: THE RIGHT OF NECESSITY AS RESPECT FOR NATURAL EQUITY

The scholastic or medieval natural law tradition, of which Aquinas was the culmination, sought to show that God had implanted in all human beings certain characteristics and tendencies that we could come to know through our rationality, in accordance with Christian revelation (which, in turn, helped us to further our knowledge of the law). Early modern natural law theorists do not dispute that God is at the origin of natural law, but seek to give a secular account of how we come to know this law, so that we could accept its existence even if there were no God, or even if God did not care for human affairs.[29] This goal was sensible given the circumstances: living in Protestant countries after the Reformation, those who subscribed to this tradition were confronted not only with divisive religious wars within Christian Europe but also with a world increasingly open to trade and relations with other countries and cultures, whose ways of living seemed to differ with theirs on everything except some bare essentials. In this context, the quest for a basic, minimal moral order given by nature and shared by all human beings regardless of their creed is what distinguishes Hugo Grotius's project (1583–1645) and earns him his reputation as one of the founding fathers of the early modern natural law tradition.[30]

Reacting to the Hobbesian view where individuals are purely self-interested creatures who come to live together and to respect moral rules purely for their own security and benefit, Grotius opts for a more balanced moral psychology, where humans are taken to be naturally self-interested but also naturally sociable. Starting from this assumption, he then constructs a genealogy of civil society. In order to understand Grotius's account of the right of necessity, it is first required to say something about this genealogy and about his conception of the origins and function of property rights within it.

From Common Use to Property Rights

In continuity with his medieval predecessors, Grotius agrees that in the original state of nature (which he conceives as real), we shared the fruits of the earth in common: 'All things, as Justin says, "were the common and undivided possession of all men, as if all possessed a common inheritance." In consequence, each man could at once take whatever he wished for his own needs, and could consume whatever was capable of being consumed'.[31] All human beings thus stand in an original footing of equality regarding the use of the earth's resources; an original footing that gives us a 'kind of moral independence from one another' that is never relinquished.[32]

Grotius uses Cicero's example of a public theatre, where spectators freely come in and take a vacant seat, as analogous to the original state of common use: although nobody owns any seat *in particular*, once they have chosen one they can properly say that they have a right to it. But this right is limited to the use of the seat for as long as they stay, and is extinguished when they stand up and leave. It is then neither *a right to a seat* that may be claimed in their presence or absence nor *a right to get a seat* if they come late and all the places are already taken. (This second option seems to have been precluded based on the tacit assumption that there are enough seats for everyone, just as the earth is assumed to have enough resources to freely satisfy the needs of all humankind.)

If we had kept living in primitive simplicity and on friendly terms with each other, things could have remained this way—as in fact happened, according to Grotius, among Native American tribes and some ascetic communities. However, as we can see from history, most of the time humans wanted to leave the caves and their lives focused on immediate, short-term subsistence. When they started adding labour and ingenuity to the common products of the earth, and when they started accumulating and storing these products, the institution of property entered into the picture, either by explicit agreement (for example, by the division of land among neighbours) or by implicit agreement (according to Grotius, first occupancy belongs in this category). Through the institution of property, men could extend their control over things that were not to be used or consumed on the spot, and this led to an improved existence where culture, industry, science and the arts could flourish. Once this was settled, it was also settled that no one could take away what belonged to someone else without violating the rules of justice. The right to property was what Grotius called a *faculty*, and what Pufendorf was later going to call a *perfect right*—namely, a right enforceable by human laws the infringement of which was punishable.[33] Thus, through the introduction of property arrangements the existence of subjective rights was established and the adjudication of rights was regulated, by developing a legal apparatus around them.

To go back to the theatre analogy, once the system of property is established, it is as though everyone agrees that from then on each person has to buy a ticket to get a seat. By buying the ticket, they acquire not only a right *to use the seat* while they are present (as used to be the case) but also a right *to this particular seat*, valid in their presence or absence. Again, the right *to get a seat*, insofar as the theatre is big enough to lodge all potential spectators, is tacitly assumed.

In spite of this, if it is ever the case that a person falls in dire need and has no other way out but to take and use what belongs to someone else, Grotius concedes that he may go ahead without being charged of theft. How can this be? Grotius understands the right of necessity as a right to use things that are part of someone else's property. This sounds contradictory, having just established that the system of private property replaces the original one of common use, turning things that were not owned by anyone into part of the extended sphere of control of particular individuals. But there is no contradiction, Grotius thinks, and the reason is the following: We have to presume that the intention of those who first agreed on instituting a system of individual ownership was to depart from natural equity as little as possible. This means that, if we interpret the original spirit in which the law was conceived (rather than blindly following the law to the letter), we have to presume that those who established property laws would have agreed to allow for this exception: that, in situations of extreme need, the system of common use revives, so that the needy person may take someone else's property as she would have done in the original state, where nothing yet belonged to anyone specifically. This explains why, under circumstances of necessity, what would normally be considered as theft ought not to be regarded as such.[34]

Against what some churchmen had argued before him, and what Pufendorf would argue later, Grotius rejects another possible justification of this right, which is that it correlates with the duty of humanity or charity to give away one's surplus to the needy. Rather, as was just said, one's duty is to acknowledge that the right of necessity should be built into the system of private property from the very beginning. This right is thus to be excepted by human laws, given that its justification is grounded on natural law—specifically, on the right of common use to which all human beings are equally entitled and which serves as an internal limitation to all property arrangements.

A Mere Privilege?

It might appear that the right of necessity thus described and the right of common use, of which the first is a revival, are what in Hohfeldian terminology are called *privileges.* According to Hohfeld, when A has a privilege to φ (where φ is an action), A has no duty not to φ. A privilege to φ is thus the absence of a duty of opposite content. Moreover, having the privilege to φ neither prejudges whether A also has a duty to φ nor prejudges whether B, C, D, and so on have a duty not to interfere with A's φing. That A has a privilege to do something consequently leaves open the question whether others have or do not have a duty to let her go ahead.[35]

In the original state, before any agreements have been made, Grotius envisions every individual as having a privilege to take and use whatever he needs to preserve himself—for example, picking a mango from the mango tree nearby. This means that A is free to pick the mango—that is, she has no duty not to pick it. Because privileges do not entail any correlated duties on others, however, in principle A has no claim against B, C, D, and so on not to interfere with her picking the mango.

In a world where resources are abundant, where people live simple lives, and where they are more or less on friendly terms with each other (which is how Grotius depicts the state of nature), one can see how this might work. Whenever she gets hungry, A goes to the closest mango tree and grabs a fruit for her immediate consumption, with a reasonable expectation that she will not be hindered by others. After all, *ex hypothesi* there are enough mangoes readily available for anyone to take, so it seems unlikely that B, C, D, and so on will interfere with A picking the fruit she wants.

But there is an obvious problem with understanding the right of necessity and the right of common use as mere privileges—namely, it makes the use and consumption of those things that belong in the original community dependent at best on the good will of the participants, and at worst on their brute force and skill. If A has no claim against B, C, D, and so on not to interfere with her picking the mango, they may indeed prevent her from so doing by picking it themselves—something that will be relatively easy to do if they are stronger, faster and more dextrous.

Commenting on Grotius's proposal, John Salter offers the following solution. Taking the example of the public theatre, one might say that the privilege of the citizens to get a free seat owes its existence to the total absence of claims to seats, but also to 'the fact that citizens possess the right not to be physically assaulted on their way to the theatre or to be physically evicted from their seats once they have occupied them'.[36] In other words, Salter implies that the privilege of common use works in conjunction with the *claim* that every individual has against others to keep his bodily integrity. Others are allowed, then, to run faster than me and get the seats with the best views, so long as they do not harm me in the process, and so long as they do not interfere with my trying to get a seat. Moreover, supplementing the bare privilege of common use by a proper claim against others to the things that one has already brought under one's possession prevents newcomers from evicting spectators who are already seated: doing otherwise would be considered physical aggression and, thereby, an attack against one's own sovereign sphere, to which one could respond by employing force against the aggressors. In the mango example, supplementing the privilege to pick a fruit with the claim to things that one has already brought under one's possession means that other parties are prevented from taking the mango from my mouth, and presumably also from my hands, when I am about to take a bite out of it.

Although Salter does not draw this conclusion, what this suggests is that, even in the original state of common use, there must already be a tacit agreement that we do not merely have a *privilege* but also a *claim* against other people to those external things that are under our possession for our immediate use and/or consumption.[37] Grotius only says something very brief along these lines—namely, that 'whatever each had thus taken for his own needs another could not take from him except by an unjust act'.[38] The equal privilege that others have to pick the mango seems to end, then, as soon as I have grabbed it.[39]

As Karl Olivecrona has put it, before conventional property arrangements enter the picture, there already seem to be some things that belong to every person: what Grotius, and later Pufendorf, call the *suum* (literally in Latin, *his/their*; a person's own).[40] Rather than a definition or a conceptual analysis of the term, Grotius offers a list of things that constitute the basic *suum*: 'one's life, body, limbs, reputation, honor, sexual integrity, and one's actions. Added to this are the things necessary for one's safety'.[41] The word 'denotes the realm over which the individual is sovereign'[42] and is of key importance in Grotius's theory and in modern natural law theory in general, delimiting the moral sphere of each individual, encroachment upon which is an injustice and therefore justifies the use of force.

In civil society, the *suum* is extended to the things over which one acquires conventional property rights, be it through promises, contracts, and so on and so forth. In this new setting, it is not the individuals by their own hands but the legal system which is in charge of protecting the *suum* of its citizens, and correcting and punishing any trespasses. The right to protect one's *suum*, however, is never entirely relinquished, and in exceptional circumstances individuals may resort to it to preserve themselves. The right of necessity is an expression of this kind of situation. Being a revival of the right of common use, it permits the person to take measures conducive to her survival—that is, to the preservation of her most basic *suum*, when there is no other way to ensure this. That is why she may treat other people's material resources as if they were yet common.

There are two important omissions in Grotius's account of the right of necessity as a revival of the right of common use. First, nothing is said about what the owners of the resources needed and other parties should do when confronted with a person exercising this right. Apart from denying that the justification of this right is the duty of charity towards those in need, Grotius is dead silent regarding the morally correct attitude or course of action for those whose property is being taken, used and/or occupied, and for other potential spectators on the scene. Second, Grotius never mentions the use of force as an option if this happens to be the only way in which the needy may access the resources in question. He suggests that necessity gives persons the freedom in the form of a privilege to go after the property of others, but nothing is said as to what the person is supposed to do if the owners of the property needed (or others) interfere with her actions. This would seem to indicate that Grotius rejects the use of force by the needy against the owners, and also against others.

These two omissions leave open the question of what Grotius really meant by saying that the right of necessity was a revival of the right of common use. There are two possibilities, neither of which seems satisfactory. One is that, under necessity, only the needy person normatively retreats to the state of common use, while everything else stays equal. If this is the case, however, then the owner of the targeted resources (and anyone else, for that matter) may interfere with the needy's actions, from the moment when she sets to look for the needed resources to the moment when she is about to consume them. If the right of necessity meant just this, it would be pretty toothless—as toothless as a sort of game that Hohfeld describes, where the owners of a salad grant a privilege to someone else to eat it, while retaining their claim over it:

> A, B, C and D, being the owners of the salad, might say to X: 'Eat the salad, if you can; you have our license to do so, but we don't agree not to interfere with you'. In such a case the privileges exist, so that if X succeeds in eating the salad, he has violated no rights [in the sense of claims] of any of the parties. But it is equally clear that if A had succeeded in holding so fast to the dish that X couldn't eat the contents, no right [in the sense of claim] of X would have been violated.[43]

A second possibility is that, under necessity, not only the needy person but also the owner of the resources needed are normatively back in the state of common use. If this is what Grotius means, then the needy and the owner have an equal privilege to bring the required resources under their possession, and whoever gets hold of them first acquires a claim against the other. In this reading, if the owner repossesses the needed object first, then the needy has nothing to complain about. This scenario also looks like a game, where the owner says to the needy, 'I give up the claim over my property, so that now we can compete as equals to get it. If I lose, you may take what was part of my extended *suum* and use it as you will, but if I win, you have no claim whatsoever against my using it, even if you starve as a result'. What counts against this interpretation is that Grotius never says that the needy may force the owner to abstain from interfering with her actions—something that follows if the right of necessity is understood as a privilege plus a claim of non-interference against others. Against Grotius's contention that the right of necessity is simply a retreat to the original right of common use, there thus seems to be this important asymmetry between the two: while in the latter those who have taken possession of something may defend it even by force, such conduct does not seem available in the former.

Three Admonitions

Most of the time and in most situations, morality dictates that property rights should be respected. It is only in cases of dire need when the right of necessity kicks in and reminds us, as it were, of the internal limitation of property rights, set by virtue of the original moral equality in which we stand in the state of common use. This is, in a nutshell, Grotius's argument. Thereafter, Grotius sets up three *admonitions* for those invoking necessity.

The first admonition is that the right only holds 'when the necessity is in no way avoidable'—that is, when the person has already tried, albeit unsuccessfully, to get out of her plight by other means: 'every effort should be made to see whether the necessity can be avoided in any other way, as, for example, by appealing to a magistrate, or even by trying through entreaties to obtain the use of the thing from the owner'.[44] This admonition, which echoes what I call the *last resort condition,* is repeated by every single author writing on this topic. This is not surprising: given the disruptive potential of such a moral prerogative, those who agree to leave a conceptual and practical space for it are at the same time cautious, wanting to make sure that it will not be misused or abused, creating more of a problem than a solution. In Grotius's case, this is taken to the extreme that he does not even object to slavery if the point is to have the necessaries of life secured in exchange.[45]

Second, the right of necessity only holds when the owner of the thing required is not himself under equal need. Three different arguments are offered by Grotius to justify this limitation. The first comes from Lactantius, an early Christian scholar, who appeals to the idea that it is preferable to jeopardise one's own safety rather than hurt another and thus be guilty of sin. The second comes from Cicero, who denies that one has a right to steal the food from 'someone of no account' and affirms in Stoical mode that the state of mind that prevents us from so doing is to be valued more than our own lives. The third argument is from the Roman historian Curtius, who is quoted saying that '[t]he man who will not part with his own has a better case than the man who demands what belongs to another'.[46]

Considering that Grotius purports to give a secular account of morality that may be accepted by everyone regardless of their creed, one would do better to leave the first argument aside. Regarding Cicero's argument, at first sight it seems to make sense to appeal to it, given the importance that both the Stoics and the early natural law thinkers assign to honour and reputation. Insofar as these are part of the basic *suum*, it is easier to see why it would be preferable to starve rather than to take from someone as needy as oneself. The problem with this way of arguing is that it sets an absolute rather than a relative prescription, leaving the possibility of claiming necessity completely out of the question, regardless of whether the owner of the resources needed is equally needy.

Curtius's argument is the one that best suits Grotius's purposes, so long as what belongs to another is understood as meaning one's minimal, rather than one's extended *suum*. If someone is as needy as I am, probably all that he has is already under his possession and for his immediate consumption. And, as was said above, because any encroachment upon his bodily integrity would be a violation of his *suum* (an action to which he could respond by using force), dispossessing him would be wronging him and committing an injustice. The privilege of necessity is therefore tempered by each person's claim to their basic *suum*. This, moreover, would serve as a response to Pufendorf's complaint against Grotius that 'if necessity gives a man a right of seizing on the goods of others, what hinders that, if he have sufficient strength, he may take from the owners, when they are at the same time pinched with the like necessity'?[47] Whereas this critique hits the target if the right of necessity is understood merely as a privilege (where might makes right), it doesn't if we bear in mind that this privilege must always be supplemented by a claim against others not to interfere with what lies already in one's possession.

The third and final admonition given by Grotius to exercise the right of necessity is that restitution of the thing used is due to its owner whenever possible. Grotius justifies restitution on the grounds that 'it is nearer the truth to say, that the right here was not absolute, but was restricted by the burden of making restitution, where necessity allowed'.[48] But this leads to a counterargument: there must be restitution because the right of necessity is not an absolute right but a right restricted by a duty of restitution!

This third admonition is indeed difficult to justify if one understands the right of necessity as a retreat to the right of common use. If, on the one hand, one takes this right to be merely a privilege, then it may not be a bad idea to show gratitude towards those who, having no correlated duties not to interfere, yet abstain from so doing. But there is a long way from making what is commendable into something obligatory. If, on the other hand, one interprets the Grotian right of necessity as a privilege plus a claim against others to the things one possesses, then restitution does not seem to fit at all. As Pufendorf remarks, why should one be obliged to restitute what is one's due?[49]

One way out of the conundrum would be to elaborate on the story of the original agreement through which we entered into civil society, and explain why the right of necessity should be accepted so long as a restitution clause came attached to it. Along these lines, one could argue that demanding restitution diminishes moral hazard in two ways: it discourages a frivolous use of the principle (invoking necessity is less attractive if one has to pay back), and it preserves the incentive to save and accumulate (by guaranteeing to the owners that, whenever possible, they will get back what was taken away from them). Although this sounds plausible, it is only a guess of what Grotius could have said, but did not.

CONCLUDING REMARKS

In this chapter, I presented an account of the right of necessity as a retreat to the original right of common use of the earth's resources. This was the view developed by Christian canonists and theologians from the end of the twelfth century onward, and later secularised by Hugo Grotius.

Regarding the medieval accounts of the right of necessity, the most prominent of which is Aquinas's, I suggested that one can find in them all the main features that reappear in later theorists: the right is universal; it is triggered by serious need, regardless of its origin and of its duration; it may be exercised even against the will of the owner of the targeted resources, openly or secretly, but only as a last resort; it is a transitive right that may be exercised by third parties on behalf of the needy, and it is not conceived as conflicting with property rights, but rather as constituting an in-built limitation of the latter. While widely accepted in the moral and theological realms, however, I pointed out how the exercise of this right by the chronically deprived was hardly ever tolerated by civil and common law.

I then presented Grotius's position as a secularisation of the medieval version of the right of necessity. Introducing the Hohfeldian typology of incidents of rights, I suggested that understanding the Grotian right of common use as a mere privilege is problematic, and proposed to interpret it instead as a privilege compounded with a claim of non-interference against others to those things brought under one's possession and required for one's subsistence. The problem with this interpretation, however, is that it doesn't sit comfortably with Grotius's presentation of the right of necessity as a revival of the right of common use. If the right of necessity were exactly that, then the needy person would have a claim against the owner of the resources targeted once she came to possess them, a claim that she could defend by force, something that Grotius never implies, and the owner in turn would have a duty to let the needy use his property as if it were yet common, a duty which is also completely absent from Grotius's account. Moreover, I pointed to three admonitions that Grotius sets for the exercise of this right and suggested that the justification of two of them (that is, the requirement of restitution and the prohibition not to take from those equally needy) require giving arguments that Grotius fails to give.

I also underlined Grotius's justification of the right of necessity on the idea of natural equity—namely, that it is reasonable to presume that those who first instituted property laws would have allowed for this exceptional moral prerogative in situations where following the law to the letter would go against the very reasons for which it was instituted in the first place. As will be seen in the next chapter, this rationale is echoed by Pufendorf and constitutes, in my view, a solid foundation for the right of necessity that sets it in continuity, rather than opposition, with property rights.

NOTES

1. Historical accounts of the right of necessity are given by Stephen Buckle, *Natural Law and the Theory of Property: Grotius to Hume* (New York: Clarendon Press, 1991); Samuel Fleischacker, *A Short History of Distributive Justice* (Cambridge, MA: Harvard University Press, 2004), 28–34, and Scott G. Swanson, 'The Medieval Foundations of John Locke's Theory of Natural Rights: Rights of Subsistence and the Principle of Extreme Necessity', *History of Political Thought* 18, 3 (1997): 400–458.

2. See Alasdair MacIntyre, *Whose Justice? Which Rationality?* (Notre Dame: University of Notre Dame Press, 1988), 370ff. See also Quentin Skinner's claim that old works of political theory cannot be read straightforwardly as contributions to long-lasting debates of political ideas: Quentin Skinner, 'Meaning and Understanding in the History of Ideas', *History and Theory* 8, 1 (1969): 3–53.

3. The factual assumption that there is a basic global economic structure in which we all partake is obviously absent among these authors, but it can easily be incorporated without affecting their main arguments.

4. Francis Hutcheson, *A Short Introduction to Moral Philosophy*, ed. Luigi Turco (Indianapolis: Liberty Fund, 2007), XVI.1, 206.

5. Hutcheson, *System* II.XVII.9, 139. The example he chooses is that of an 'innocent man' who takes the neighbor's horse to escape an unjust murderer (Hutcheson, *System* II.XVII.4, 123, and II.III.11, 274). Hutcheson's treatment of necessity is thus much more

congenial to one of the dominant interpretations of necessity in the common law, where it normally refers to cases where what is at stake is the greater good of society. See Robinson, 'Criminal Law Defenses', 213.

6. Locke, *First Treatise* I.§42, 170.

7. Locke, *First Treatise* I.§42, 170. Cf. Jeremy Shearmur, 'The Right to Subsistence in a "Lockean" State of Nature', *Southern Journal of Philosophy* 27 (1989), who does interpret Locke as giving the needy a right to take matters into their own hands.

8. Quoted in Aquinas, *Summa* II-II, Question 32, Article 5, 385 and 216.

9. See, for example, Robert L. Benson and Giles Constable, *Renaissance and Renewal in the Twelfth Century* (Cambridge, MA: Harvard University Press, 1982).

10. For the concept of *negative community*, see Pufendorf, *The Law of Nature and Nations (DJN)*, IV.IV.2–3, 356–57, and IV.IV.13, 375–76.

11. Swanson, 'The Medieval Foundations', 409.

12. Quoted in Brian Tierney, *The Idea of Natural Rights* (Atlanta: Scholars Press, 1997), 72.

13. Swanson, 'The Medieval Foundations', 408.

14. Aristotle, *Nicomachean Ethics*, ed. Jonathan Barnes, vol. 2, *The Complete Works of Aristotle* (Princeton, NJ: Princeton University Press, 1984), 1107a1–10, 748.

15. Aquinas, *Summa* II-II, Question 66, Article 7.

16. Aquinas, *Summa* II-II, Question 66, Article 7.

17. Aquinas understood private property as giving individuals a power to manage and dispense of external things. He considered it a necessary institution for three reasons. First, because we are more careful to look after things that belong to us than after things that are common to all or many. Second, because human affairs are better and more orderly handled when every person has something under her own care. And third, because peace is better ensured in a society where each person has his own lot, rather than in one where things are possessed jointly. Aquinas, *Summa* II-II, Question 66, Article 2, 54–55.

18. Much more could be said regarding the understanding of the right of necessity as a duty towards God. Given that what I am trying to offer is a secularised version of this right, I leave this topic aside on the belief that the implications that should be drawn from a theologically derived account of necessity would be, if anything, stronger than the ones here suggested.

19. Cf., for example, John Rickaby's notes commenting this passage of the *Summa* in Thomas Aquinas, *Aquinas Ethicus*, ed. Joseph Rickaby, vol. 2 (London: Burns and Oates, 1892), 58.

20. Quoted in Virpi Mäkinen, 'Rights and Duties in Late Scholastic Discussion on Extreme Necessity', in *Transformations in Medieval and Early Modern Rights Discourse*, ed. Virpi Mäkinen and Petter Korkman (Dordrecht: Springer, 2006), 44.

21. All quoted in Brian Tierney, 'Origins of Natural Rights Language: Texts and Contexts, 1150–1250', *History of Political Thought* 10 (1989): 642.

22. When discussing almsgiving, Aquinas tacitly adds another condition to the exercise of the right of necessity: 'if a man found himself in the presence of a case of urgency, and had merely sufficient to support himself and his children, or others under his charge, he would be throwing away his life and that of others if he were to give away in alms, what was then necessary to him' (Aquinas, *Summa*, Question 32, Article 6). This looks like the limitation later explicitly stated by Grotius and Pufendorf that one may not take from those who are in a similar situation of need.

23. During the late thirteenth and early fourteenth centuries, the principle of necessity also received much attention in the context of the debate surrounding the Franciscan ideal of total renunciation to earthly goods. On the one hand, the Franciscans claimed that they had given up all their rights to property, and only kept a *use of fact* over things necessary for survival. On the other hand, Pope John XXII rebutted that, in order to use things that were consumed by such use, some sort of *property* over them was first required. Settling this question was important given that, for those opposing the Franciscan position, complying with one's duty towards God to stay alive required

that one had a certain *property* in common goods that could not be renounced. For extended discussion, see John Kilcullen, 'The Origin of Property: Ockham, Grotius, Pufendorf, and Some Others', 1995, accessed August 10, 2015, http://www.mq.edu.au/about_us/faculties_and_departments/faculty_of_arts/mhpir/staff/staff-politics_and_international_relations/john_kilcullen/the_origin_of_property_ockham_grotius_pufendorf_and_some_others/; and Virpi Mäkinen, 'Individual Natural Rights in the Discussion on Franciscan Poverty', *Studia Theologica* 53 (1999), and Mäkinen, 'Rights and Duties', 46ff.

24. Swanson, 'The Medieval Foundations', 401.

25. Åke Holmbäck and Elias Wessén, eds., *Svenska Landskapslagar: Tolkade Och Förklarade För Nutidens Svenskar*, vol. 3 (Uppsala: Hugo Gebers Förlag, 1940). I thank Virpi Mäkinen for pointing me to this reference.

26. Siegfried Van Duffel and Dennis Yap, 'Distributive Justice before the Eighteenth Century: The Right of Necessity', *History of Political Thought* 32, 3 (2011): 458.

27. Tierney, *The Idea of Natural Rights*, 74. See also Brian Tierney, *Medieval Poor Law: A Sketch of Canonical Theory and Its Application in England* (Berkeley: University of California Press, 1959), 13.

28. Against Samuel Fleischacker, who underlines that the right of necessity was conceived as neither part of the normal course of events nor an institutionalisable right (Fleischacker, *Short History*, 28–34), Siegfried Van Duffel and Dennis Yap have stretched the historical evidence a bit too far, in my view, to suggest that 'protection of the right of necessity was enforced and it did provide a basis for state-guaranteed distribution of basic necessities': Van Duffel and Yap, 'Distributive Justice', 463–64.

29. This is a paraphrase of Grotius's famous *etiamsi daremus passage*, for which he was later deemed as the great seculariser: 'What we have been saying would have a degree of validity even if we should concede that which cannot be conceded without the utmost wickedness, that there is no God or that the affairs of men are of no concern to Him'. Grotius, *The Law of War and Peace (DJB), Prolegomena* §11, 13.

30. Contemporary Grotians have underlined Grotius's quest for a minimal global morality. See, for example, Mathias Risse, who claims that Grotius develops a standpoint of *global public reason*, seeking to justify his position by giving reasons that may be accepted by people from different cultural, political and religious backgrounds. Mathias Risse, *On Global Justice* (Princeton, NJ: Princeton University Press, 2012), 90.

31. Grotius, *DJB* II.II.2, 186.

32. Dennis Klimchuk, 'Property and Necessity', in *Philosophical Foundations of Property Law*, ed. James Penner and Henry Smith (Oxford: Oxford University Press, 2013), 53.

33. *Faculties* are contrasted with *aptitudes*, regulated by the rules of love and never to be enforced. Grotius, *DJB* I.I.4–7, 35–37.

34. *DJB* II.II.6, 195. Grotius starts with classic examples of one-off emergencies: 'On a voyage, if provisions fail, whatever each person has ought to be contributed to the common stock. Thus, again, if fire has broken out, in order to protect a building belonging to me I can destroy a building of my neighbor. I can, furthermore, cut the ropes or nets in which my ship has been caught, if it cannot otherwise be freed'. He then adds, somehow aloofly, the cases of chronic deprivation discussed by medieval authors: 'Even among the theologians the principle has been accepted that, if a man under stress of such necessity takes from the property of another what is necessary to preserve his own life, he does not commit a theft'. Grotius, *DJB* II.II.VI, 193.

35. Hohfeld, 'Fundamental Legal Conceptions', 36. Wesley Newcomb Hohfeld (1879–1918) was an American jurist who made an important contribution to our current understanding of the concept of rights. Noticing that different meanings of the word *right* got conflated and confused all the time in the practice of the law, he set out to analyse rights in terms of four different incidents: *claims, privileges, powers* and *immunities*. While Hohfeld's analysis was done at the judicial level, many moral philosophers have taken these categories and applied them to classify moral rights. I join them here.

36. John Salter, 'Grotius and Pufendorf on the Right of Necessity', *History of Political Thought* 26, 2 (2005), 288. See also John Salter, 'Hugo Grotius: Property and Consent', *Political Theory* 29, 4 (2001).

37. As Pufendorf would later put it, this constitutes the basic agreement of *primitive seizure*: 'that what any person had seized out of the common store of things, or out of the fruits of them, with design to apply to his own private occasions, none else should rob him of'. Pufendorf, *DJN* IV.IV.5, 366. See also 'The first convention among mortals is understood to have been to the effect that if someone had taken possession of things with the intention of making use of them, nobody should take them from him. If there had been no such convention, men would have had to abstain from using anything at all': Karl Olivecrona, 'Appropriation in the State of Nature: Locke on the Origin of Property', *Journal of the History of Ideas* 35, 2 (1974): 217.

38. Grotius, *DJB* II.II.1, 186.

39. More recently, Mathias Risse has suggested that this right is no mere *privilege*, but must be supplemented by what H. L. A. Hart called a 'protective perimeter of *claims rights*'. Furthermore, Risse adds that this right also works as an *immunity*—that is, 'a right not to be subject to economic and political conditions under which the goals which are supposed to be secured by these rights can no longer be secured' (Risse, *On Global Justice*, 101). I am sympathetic to Risse's reading of the right of common use as providing an individual immunity against a societal order that impedes direct access to resources and spaces to satisfy one's basic needs, while impeding, at the same time, opportunities to satisfy those basic needs in some other way. I think, however, that it is too speculative to attribute such thoughts to Grotius, who never points to anything along these lines either explicitly or implicitly. As I claim in the next chapter, Pufendorf seems to have come much closer to vindicating such an immunity—although, of course, he did not phrase it in this language, and he did not found it in the right of common use, but rather in the right to self-preservation.

40. Karl Olivecrona, 'The Two Levels in Natural Law Thinking', trans. Thomas Mautner, *Jurisprudence* 2 (2010): 210.

41. Thomas Mautner, 'Introduction: A Lawless Natural Law', to Karl Olivecrona, 'The Two Levels in Natural Law Thinking', 203. See also Thomas Mautner, 'Pufendorf and 18th-Century Scottish Philosophy', *Samuel von Pufendorf 1632–1982. Ett Rättshistoriskt Symposium i Lund* (Lund: Bloms Boktryckeri AB, 1982), 123.

42. Mautner, 'Introduction', 202.

43. Hohfeld, 'Fundamental Legal Conceptions', 35.

44. Grotius, *DJB* II.II.6, 194–95.

45. I think this uncritical acceptance of slavery directly contradicts Grotius's idea of a minimal morality of equals, and results from his historical method of resorting to ancient writers and sources to then draw conclusions about things that are right or wrong by nature. Pufendorf and Rousseau would later harshly criticise this method of trying to derive permanent truths from culturally laden and uncritically received customs and prejudices. See Grotius, *DJB* I.III.8 and II.V.27.

46. Quoted in Grotius, *DJB* II.II.8, 194–95.

47. Pufendorf, *DJN* II.VI.6, 208.

48. Grotius, *DJB* II.II.6, 195.

49. Pufendorf, *DJN* II.VI.6, 208.

THREE

The Right of Necessity and the Pull of Self-Preservation

Familiar to some for his pioneering contributions to international law, the moral and political theory of Samuel Pufendorf (1632–1694) has only recently started to capture the attention it deserves.[1] During his lifetime and for over half a century after his death, notwithstanding, he was one of the most popular and widely read philosophers of his time, having his major work, *Of the Law of Nature and Nations* (*DJN*, 1672), reprinted several times and translated into all the main European languages.[2]

Pufendorf follows Grotius's footsteps when it comes to offering a systematic account of natural law that does not rely on religious creed, but on secular and non-metaphysical grounds. Through the observation of human nature and through reason, Pufendorf thinks, we can derive the main tenets of this law, and the main duties and rights derived therefrom. Still, God does come into the picture to give its obligatory nature to the law: a moral voluntarist, Pufendorf does not think that a rational understanding and knowledge of the law give reason enough to follow it. If we are compelled to it, it is because the law is the command of a superior who has authority over us and the power to sanction us, and to whom we are tied with a moral bond. Despite this, as Karl Olivecrona has suggested, it is plausible to affirm that important parts of Pufendorf's theory (as well as Grotius's) can function independently of any divine intervention, insofar as his account of moral rights and duties is based on a pre-existing natural order. In what follows, I interpret Pufendorf along these lines and leave aside the question of whether a theory of natural law so conceived can motivate individuals to act morally.[3]

In this chapter, I examine Pufendorf's basic moral tenets, together with his division of rights and duties into perfect and imperfect, his genealogy of property rights, and the justificatory role played by the natural pull of self-preservation within his account of the right of necessity. For someone who emphatically underlines the importance of preserving political and social stability through the respect of the law (paradigmatically, property laws), the granting of this right to those who are in a deprived situation might sound incongruous—and all the more considering that, contra Grotius and Aquinas, Pufendorf does explicitly see this right as correlating with an enforceable duty of humanity of those who are able to help. My aim is to show, however, that behind his seeming inconsistencies lies a visionary account of what individuals may minimally demand from any institutional system if they are to subject themselves to its rules.

PERFECT AND IMPERFECT RIGHTS AND DUTIES

For Pufendorf, the most basic and evident fact about human nature is our anxious desire of self-preservation, which we share with other animals and is so strong that it leads us to resort to all sorts of means to secure it. Unlike other animals, however, we are too feeble to preserve ourselves without the aid of others, while at the same time we are prone to harming each other and to do mischief. The 'wonderful impotency and human indigence' in which we find ourselves in the natural state, coupled with our strong desire of self-preservation, give rise to the first principle of the law of nature: that 'every man ought, as far as in him lies, to promote and preserve a peaceful sociableness with others, agreeable to the main end and disposition of human race in general'.[4]

Sociability is, then, the most fundamental prescription of the law of nature, and our duties to ourselves and to others derive from it. Depending on their source, these duties are divided into absolute and hypothetical or conditional. Absolute duties, as opposed to hypothetical or conditional ones, oblige us as human beings, independently of any compacts or arrangements. They are basically three: not to harm others, to treat them as equals and to benefit them as much as we can. Depending on their form, moreover, duties can be perfect or imperfect. Compliance with perfect duties '[c]onduces to the very being' of society and 'may be required and executed by more severe courses and means'. Imperfect duties, on the contrary, are not indispensable for the very *being* of society, but for its *well-being*, so that 'it is mere folly to require a remedy more grievous than the disease'.[5] This last phrase points to the idea that attempts to enforce imperfect duties will generally be oppressive and do a disservice to the end they are trying to promote.

Accordingly, duties not to harm others are classified by Pufendorf as perfect, while duties to promote their good are imperfect. The former are 'a guard and fence to those things which we receive from the immediate hand of nature, as our life, our bodies, our members, our chastity, our reputation, and our liberty; engaging men to keep them sacred and inviolable'. Their primary objective, then, is the protection of the basic *suum* (note the similarities between Pufendorf's and Grotius's lists). Provided that we do not trespass into each other's sovereign sphere, we can live together 'under some tolerable comfort and quiet'. This is all we normally request from the rest of society, while the beneficial effects of charity, generosity and compassion we only expect from a few.[6] Once in civil society, perfect rights and duties cover also our extended *suum* (i.e., our property) so that transgressions into it are considered as violations of a perfect duty, and are therefore punishable by law.

But no matter how conceivable it is to have a society where individuals merely abstain from encroaching into one another's *suum* without further relating to each other, Pufendorf does not think this is enough to comply with the precept of sociability. In order to fulfil it, we have to further the good of our fellow-beings through the performance of 'the common duties of humanity'.[7] It has been suggested that this is one of Pufendorf's contributions to modern natural law; to wit, 'to have transformed the weak notion of sociability in the Grotian tradition into a much stronger notion of human mutual aid'.[8] Based on the old Ciceronian account of duties of beneficence, Pufendorf offers a full gradation of these, from the easiest acts of kindness (like giving directions to a lost traveller or allowing someone the use of running water) to those the performance of which is more costly and the exercise of which shows a greater moral worth (like liberality, gratitude and hospitality). Because we have only an imperfect right to these kinds of acts, it is neither proper to feel injured by those who fail to perform them nor permissible to exact this performance by force. But there is one exception to this rule. That is where the right of necessity enters into the picture.

PROPERTY AND NECESSITY

One of the big changes brought about by the emergence of civil society and property arrangements is that individuals are able to extend their *suum* to external things other than those minimally required to preserve themselves. In this new scenario,

> every man is obliged to suffer another, who is not a declared enemy, to enjoy whatsoever things are his; and neither by fraud or violence to spoil, embezzle or convert them to his own use. Whence it appears, that theft, rapine, removing of boundaries, and the like crimes, which tend to the invading and encroaching upon other men's properties, are forbidden.[9]

While in the natural state it is permissible to kill someone who tries to take away one's minimal possessions (as 'without things necessary we cannot keep ourselves alive'[10]), in civil society this is no longer allowed, and it is the civil authorities and institutions that have the right—and duty—to act on one's behalf. *Suum* violators are thus brought to the courts of justice instead, and it is only in exceptional situations (for example, when one is attacked by 'highway men and night-robbers', so that there is no time to receive protection, or one cannot expect to bring them to justice) that self-help is granted.[11]

Pufendorf highlights two reasons for establishing the institution of property. The first is to avoid the quarrels and feuds that sooner or later arise in a state of nature. No matter how peaceful small communities may be, he thinks that, as they grow larger, people put more effort and ingenuity towards improving their quality of life and it is not possible to keep the precept of human sociability unless we assign to each property rights over things. The second reason is to promote industriousness. For Pufendorf, one of the duties that we have towards ourselves (and which is founded upon the first precept of sociability) is to cultivate our abilities and endowments, pick up an activity or employment suitable to them, and become useful members of society.[12] Apart from contributing to this end, the establishment of property arrangements produces mutual advantages and gains, and ultimately serves to improve the situation of the vast majority. As Stephen Buckle points out, this is one of the first social theories to emphasise the benefits of industriousness for society, and to suggest that 'commercial society has a built-in "maximin" tendency, in that it functions steadily to improve the lot of the (non-irretrievably) worst off'.[13] Property arrangements also bring a welcome side effect for morality—namely, that men are not limited to display their assistance and charitable endeavours through the exercise of their physical strength only but may practice their common duties of humanity more extensively, disposing of their surplus at will, and making their beneficiaries obliged to them by duties of gratitude.

Not surprisingly, then, Pufendorf strongly objects to those who accumulate property without sharing it with others. This is a distortion of its original raison d'être, and the epithets used to characterise those guilty of such a failure are as strong as those used against those who are too lazy to strive for their own sustenance. In one passage, he says, 'Why should anyone undeservedly reduced to poverty, continue to want whilst you abound? Such great churls are like swine, good for nothing till they are dead'.[14] In another passage, he compares those who keep all their property to themselves with stones of irregular shape that hinder the whole frame of a building from closing together: 'those greedy churls, whose rough and savage temper inclines them to heap superfluities on themselves, and to deprive others of mere necessaries, and whose violence of passion makes them uncapable of being reclaimed ... are indeed the great impediments of society, and the plagues of mankind'.[15]

Despite this inflamed rhetoric against those who refuse to fulfil their imperfect duties of humanity, Pufendorf is adamant that, being imperfect, these duties do not obligate people in the manner that a debt would.[16] In other words, he seems to leave the relief of the needy entirely in the hands of those with the means to provide it. But there are two things that count against this interpretation: one is Pufendorf's visionary suggestion that the performance of some minimal duties of humanity should be enforced by law (i.e., turned into perfect duties) in order to prevent anyone from falling in dire need; the other is his explicit defence of the right of necessity when these provisions are not in place and the individual has no other means to get out of his plight.

To take the first one first, after emphasising the importance of respecting the owner's discretion when it comes to the fulfilment of the common duties of humanity, Pufendorf immediately adds that 'there seems to be no reason why by the additional force of a civil ordinance, it may not be turned into a strict and perfect obligation'.[17] Quoting an example from John Selden, the English jurist and scholar of ancient Jewish law, Pufendorf says that

> [this is how it was] done among the Jews: who, upon a man's refusing to give such alms as was proper for him, could force him to it by an action at law. It is no wonder, therefore, that they should forbid their poor on any account to seize on the goods of others, enjoining them to take only what private persons, or the public officers, or stewards of alms should give them on their petition. Whence the stealing of what was another's, though upon extreme necessity, passed in that state for theft or rapine.[18]

Pufendorf is here catching a glimpse of what was later to become a basic principle of the welfare state. Without saying it explicitly, he is pointing at both the need and the convenience of securing at least some minimal material provisions for all members of society, and to do this through the legal enforcement of otherwise imperfect moral duties of humanity. To our ears, it might sound strange to attribute to duties of humanity what we take today to be the mission of distributive justice. It must be borne in mind, however, the time at which Pufendorf is writing: a time when the relief of the worst off in society are still left to the charitable endeavours of individuals and the church, rather than to the organised apparatus of the state.

What Pufendorf is tacitly acknowledging is that the very existence of society depends on its securing at least the bare essentials for the self-preservation of individuals, those things without which we cannot function as human beings. Food, water, shelter and clothing belong in this category. Their provision should thus not be left to the discretionary offices of those who wish to comply with their imperfect duties to the effect of promoting the *well-being* of society (to use his own terminology) but should be secured by perfect and thereby enforceable duties if the very *being* of society is to be guaranteed. Through the promotion of industriousness, property laws bring about the desired result hopefully most of the time, as individuals are able to maintain themselves through their 'own application and labour'.[19] For those occasions when property laws fail to fulfil this function, however, 'those things necessary without which we cannot keep ourselves alive'[20] should be provided through an institutional mechanism that legally binds everyone. Bringing back the Hohfeldian typology of rights, one could say that what Pufendorf is adumbrating is the idea that, as individuals partaking in an economic order that constrains our actions, we have an *immunity* against being subject to conditions where our very self-preservation is at stake.

This is how things ought to be, but not how they are ... yet. In a society where the government makes no such provisions for those in want, where the charity of those who can afford it is insufficient to meet the needs of the poor person, and where the latter has unsuccessfully tried to provide for himself the means for his subsistence, 'must he therefore perish with famine? Or can any human institution bind me with such a force, that in case another man neglects his duty toward me, I must rather die, than recede a little from the ordinary and the regular way of acting?' Pufendorf's answer is negative. In these cases—which resemble those that actually happen in the world as he knows it—the poor person may take 'forcibly or privily' the surplus of others without contracting 'the guilt of theft'.[21] Amidst his duty-focused morality, Pufendorf thus opens a space for the right of necessity.

Self-Preservation and the Intention of the Original Legislators

> It is impossible for a man not to apply his utmost endeavour towards preserving himself ... Therefore we cannot easily conceive or suppose, such an obligation upon him, as ought to outweigh the desire of his own safety.[22]

Such is for Pufendorf the single principle from which the right of necessity springs. Because self-preservation is of so much regard for human beings, and because it is presumed that those who laid down the laws and constitutions had as their main aim the safety and convenience of humankind, 'we may suppose them, generally speaking, to have had before their eyes the weak condition of human nature; and to have reflected upon the impossibility which every man lies under, not to avoid, and to drive off, all things that aim at his destruction'.[23]

Pufendorf's justification of the right of necessity is consequently based on two pillars: on the one hand, the recognition of the value of self-preservation for all human beings; on the other hand, the recognition that the original lawmakers would have agreed on leaving a space for this exceptional prerogative amidst the standard moral and legal rules.

It is then upon the assumption about the original intentions of the first legislators that human laws should except cases of necessity. In continuity with an ancient tradition, Pufendorf sees the right of necessity not as a challenge or a threat to human laws, but as a patent expression of their limits—an expression that must be allowed for them to remain consistent with their ultimate foundation, which is natural law.[24]

The distinction between equity and dispensation helps to clarify this point. A dispensation takes place when the lawmaker decides to clear some person from the obligations of a specific law, suspending the effect of the law over her. Only those with legislative power have the grace to dispense, but the reasons must be weighty enough, to prevent a weakening of the respect for the law, and to avoid envy and resentment among the citizens. To administer equity, by contrast, is not the grace of the legislator, but the duty of the judge, a 'correction of that in which the law, by reason of its general comprehension, was deficient: or an apt interpretation of the law, by which it is demonstrated, that there be some peculiar case which is not comprised in the universal law, because if it were, some absurdity would follow'.[25] Exceptions granted for reasons of equity arise because of the infinite variety of cases and the impossibility of accommodating them all under a limited number of human rules.

Correspondingly, the right of necessity falls under the last category. Exceptions of necessity should be granted to prevent human law from receding too much from natural law, to the point where following the former would bring about a morally undesirable or even repugnant result. The duty of judges, therefore, is to recognise when the exception arises. This is why Pufendorf harshly criticises those who qualify those acting on necessity as committing theft. One of his main targets is Antonius Matthaeus II (1601–1654), a prominent German jurist who claimed that, 'we should say that a crime is committed but under pressing need'.[26] To this, Pufendorf replies that the person in need does not exercise her right to derive any gain (what would indeed constitute a crime, according to Matthaeus's definition) but does so purely to relieve her extreme distress. Pufendorf also rejects Matthaeus's contention that, when in times of famine, the suppliers refuse to give away their stores, the opening of the granaries 'must be done on the public authority of officials and, until such time as authority intervenes, whoever intending to gratify his hunger from another's supplies takes something fraudulently will be committing a theft'.[27] Against this, Pufendorf replies that, if the authorities neglect their duties towards the hungry (in this case, by failing to order those who have the store to sell at a fair price, or to enforce redistribution), the latter are under no duty to starve and may open the granaries and help themselves to the food.

An Enforceable Duty of Humanity

Contrasted to Grotius's silence regarding both the content of the duty that correlates to the right of necessity and the acceptability of the use of force by the needy when exercising their right, Pufendorf has quite a lot to say on both fronts. From his earliest works, he underlines the active role to be played by the owner of the resources needed. On the basis of the law of humanity, 'any whatsoever is bound, when not under an equal necessity, to the extent of his power to come to the aid of a second person placed in an extreme necessity'.[28] When confronted with someone in need, humanity demands that we do something about it, either through our direct involvement (as when we can easily save someone from drowning) or through material aid (when the other is in extreme want).

Actually, it is in cases of extreme want (i.e., the cases of necessity under examination here), where our duties of humanity manifest themselves most clearly. This is because, as was said before, the establishment of property laws normally brings along a material abundance that allows individuals to practice these duties more extensively. The point of dividing external goods is not that 'every person should sit idly brooding over the share of wealth he had got, without assisting or serving his fellows'[29] but, on the contrary, to secure our own advantage and gain while furthering our mutual ties. If the owner of the resources needed does sit and brood idly over her wealth, 'the force of extreme necessity is so great, as to make these things recoverable by the same means as those which are truly and rightfully due'.[30] Confronted with the passivity or, worse, the opposition of those on whom the duty falls, 'when the necessity has merely to do with the property of the other, or when our life can be saved only by the property of the other, there is scarcely any doubt that, when no other means are available, this property can be appropriated by force, and against the will of the owner, who is not under pressure of the same necessity'.[31]

Pufendorf's conception of the right of necessity and its correlated duty of humanity is much stronger, then, than Grotius's. By virtue of what is at stake, the right of necessity changes, so to speak, the imperfect quality of an otherwise discretionary duty, turning it into one claimable by force.

Four Conditions and One Demand

Although Pufendorf founds the right of necessity on our utmost desire of self-preservation, he lays down three explicit conditions and one implicit condition for its exercise. When these are met, the owner of the targeted property acquires a duty to give it away and, if he refuses, he may be legitimately demanded to do so. The first three conditions closely echo Grotius's admonitions. First, one must appeal to the right of necessity only as a last resort—that is, 'all fairer courses are first to be tried, as complaining to the magistrate, begging and intreating, promising restitution if we are ever able, or offering to discharge the debt by equivalent labour and service'. Second, 'this license can by no means take place, when the owner of the thing which we want lies under as great a necessity as we ourselves. On the contrary, we suppose the owner to abound'. And third, 'restitution is to be made if possible; especially if the thing taken were of great value, and such as the owner could not well part without some consideration'.[32]

The fourth condition, not explicitly mentioned by Pufendorf, can be inferred both from his criticism of Grotius's account of the right of necessity and from the many examples he offers. It relates to the moral innocence of the person claiming the right, for 'how different the case is, when a man falls under such necessity by his own sloth or negligence, as when it comes on him without his fault'. For Pufendorf, that Grotius fails to consider this is a serious omission, insofar as 'a right seems to be given to idle knaves, whose vices have brought them into want, to seize forcibly for their own use the fruits of other men's honest labors'. If moral innocence is not required, these idle knaves will have no incentive to work and leave their abject condition, thus putting a permanent strain on the laborious, who will be forced to feed 'such useless bellies for nothing'![33]

The following passage condenses the conditions that the right-holder is required to fulfil, the moral duty that correlates to the right, and the consequences that failing on this duty can bring for the duty-bearer:

> If a man, not through his own fault, happens to be in extreme want of victuals and clothes necessary to preserve him from the cold, and cannot procure them from those who are wealthy and have great store, either by intreaties, or by offering their value, or by proposing to do work equivalent; he may, without being chargeable with theft or rapine, furnish his necessities out of their abundance, either by force or secretly, especially if he do so with a design to pay the price, as soon as he shall have an opportunity. For it is the duty of the opulent person to succor another who is in such a needy condition. And tho' regularly what depends upon courtesy ought by no means to be extorted by force, yet the extreme necessity alters the case, and makes these things as claimable, as if they were absolutely due by a formal obligation. But it is first incumbent upon the necessitous person to try always to supply his wants with the consent of the owner, and he is to take care that the owner be not thereby reduced to the same extremity, nor in a little time like to be so; and that restitution be made; especially if the estate of the other be such as that he cannot well bear the loss.[34]

Two worries have to be addressed here. On the one hand, if what matters morally is our instinctive pull of self-preservation, how can one require the needy to abstain from taking from the equally needy, let alone to refrain from exercising their right if they are partly or fully responsible for their diminished situation? On the other hand, regarding the demand imposed upon duty-bearers, is it not overly taxing to have to comply with one's duty of humanity each and every time one encounters a needy individual, and to be potentially subjected to the use of force if one refuses?

I suggest that the answer to both questions resides in Pufendorf's story of what the original contracting parties would have agreed to when negotiating the acceptance of the right of necessity and its correlated duty of humanity as a legitimate—as well as exceptional—limit to the standard rules of property. To be clear, this is an exegesis of what he could have replied, not what he actually said. Moreover, it is important to stress that Pufendorf's argument works against the background assumptions that owners are rightful owners, that they are not implicated in the plight of the needy, and that epistemically determining this is possible. Absent these assumptions, presumably, the principle would favour the needy even more strongly.[35]

To avoid excessively taxing potential duty-bearers, the original contractors may well have required that those claiming necessity meet these conditions. In this way, everyone in society would have an incentive to make their own living and stay above a minimal material threshold, but would also have the reassurance that, if worse came to worse, they may claim necessity against those who could help them out. In this sense, the last resort condition seems straightforward.

Regarding restitution, it could be justified along very similar lines to those offered when discussing a possible interpretation of this admonition in Grotius. For one thing, the prospect of having to compensate diminishes the incentive for people to become economically dependent on others: if one is expected to give back what one has taken, the appeal to this principle is left for cases where there is really no other way out. For another thing, by requiring that the owners be compensated, it prevents the principle from becoming overdemanding for the latter, and it preserves the individual incentive to keep working and accumulating while complying with their duty voluntarily, with the reasonable expectation that they will get back what was taken away (if not in kind, at least in grateful expressions).[36]

Regarding the requirements of moral innocence and not taking from the equally needy, these might sound especially ad hoc, given Pufendorf's insistence that it is impossible for human beings not to attempt by all means to preserve ourselves—no matter how innocent or guilty, lazy or industrious. However, as Stephen Buckle remarks in relation to the former, it is unthinkable for Pufendorf to make agents consent to a right that forces the industrious to maintain the idle and slothful at their own expense, because 'to tolerate it would transform the right of necessity from a safety net for the victims of misfortune to a manacle on social development'.[37] In fact, the cultivation of individual industriousness is such a fundamental moral trait in Pufendorf's account that, if absent, he is keen on recommending to the lazy and idle some sort of compulsory servitude, which is law-governed. This is better than self-enslavement, which he openly rejects as morally questionable, insofar as it subjects the slaves to the arbitrary will and violence of their masters and condemns the children of slaves into slavery too.[38]

In relation to the prohibition to take from the equally needy, it is easier to see why it could be part of an initial agreement between contracting parties. The right of necessity seeks to prevent anyone from falling below the minimal threshold of subsistence, and it does so through the recognition that, when not under equal necessity, others have a duty to aid those whose very self-preservation is at risk. This duty is fulfiled by letting them take, or giving to them, part of our property. However, when letting them take or giving away our property threats our own subsistence, our duty is extinguished, as is the right of necessity of others against us. After all, if this right compelled the needy to give up their own self-preservation for the sake of others equally needy, it would be trampling on the very principle it is founded upon!

Having said this, one could still ask what the non-innocent needy, as well as those who can only take from others just as needy, are supposed to do. Are they perchance to sit down and starve? Again, this is a question that Pufendorf himself does not address. A speculative answer (although one I think that he would not be dissatisfied with) is to make a distinction in treatment between cases where the agents fulfil the said conditions, and those where they do not. In the former, agents would be *justified* in their actions, while in the latter they would be merely *excused*. Accordingly, while the former would be let off the hook by the law, the latter may be asked to compensate not as a merely commendable action but as something legally due, and they may even have to respond to their deeds as a criminal offense—even though they could presumably make a plea of mitigating circumstances. Making this distinction would further discourage potential abusers or misusers of the principle.

The four conditions above mentioned ensure that the exercise of the right of necessity remains confined by strict boundaries and does not turn into a threat to social stability, by posing too heavy a demand on the other members of society—assuming, as said above, that the latter are not responsible for the plight of the needy. When these conditions are met, those on whom the claim falls have to comply with their duty by letting the needy take their resources or by directly giving it to them.

This moral demand, which may sound excessive and even outrageous to ears accustomed to the discourse of the almost inviolable right of individuals over their property, fits neatly into Pufendorf's overall moral and political theory, with its emphasis on human sociability and solidarity. To have a functioning society, it is not enough to abstain from harming others directly; sometimes helping them out is also required. Underlying this is also the idea of reciprocity, at the basis of Pufendorf's contractual argument: because they don't know whether one day they might be the party in extreme need, it makes sense for the initial contracting agents to accept that the duty of humanity in exceptional cases may be claimable as a perfect duty.

With this in mind, it is important to notice that Pufendorf gives property owners the privilege of judging whether the claimants comply with the said conditions, especially moral innocence: 'It is lawful for every proprietor to distinguish between such as are indigent out of misfortune, and such as are reduced to the same condition by their own demerit and neglect; it is plain that he has such a right over his own goods, as shall in some measure prevail even against a person in extreme necessity: so far at least as that he shall have the privilege of judging, whether the man be an object worthy of his relief or not'.[39]

At first sight, this would seem to undo with one hand what has been done with the other: What practical clout does the right of necessity retain if the needy have to rely on the judgment of others for their relief? As the quote clearly states, however, this is a privilege, and, as such, it prevails *in some measure*, not absolutely. Rather than letting the owner of the needed resources decide for the needy (or vice versa), Pufendorf ultimately lets each agent judge the moral permissibility of their own actions, which makes sense if one takes into account the epistemic limitations of each.

AN INCONGRUOUS THEORY?

In the course of his discussion of the different historical accounts of the right of necessity, Scott G. Swanson accuses Pufendorf of letting his argument

> come to rest, ark-like, on twin-peaks of contradiction ... [he] teaches that a man who fails on his obligations to succor the poor deserves to forfeit his property, but he never explains why extreme necessity entitles a person to press a claim that is not a right as though it were truly a perfect right, let alone why a magistrate might dispossess a person of something he holds by perfect right ... His theory of property rights renders claims in extreme necessity incoherent; his theory of claims in extreme necessity renders absolute property rights incoherent. He is unwilling to give up either principle, and he is incapable of resolving one principle into the other. So he simply asserts them both.[40]

But Swanson's critique rests on a twin-peak of misunderstandings. First, Pufendorf does explain why extreme necessity entitles the person to press as a perfect right something which under normal circumstances is only owed to her imperfectly: as already mentioned, it is attention to the most basic pull of self-preservation, and to the assumption that those who established the laws would have done so with this reservation—that what under normal circumstances is not enforceable becomes so under extreme necessity, allowing the agent to appeal to the relevant authorities or even to take matters into his own hands when there are no other options available. To make this prerogative as little disruptive as possible, moreover, the four conditions aforementioned have to be fulfiled by the agent pressing the claim.

Second, Swanson misunderstands the role that property rights play in Pufendorf's theory. Contrary to what he affirms, the right to property is not absolute: neither as Pufendorf understands this term nor as the term is normally understood, as something holding with no exceptions. To recall, Pufendorf defines absolute duties (and their correlative rights) as those that everyone holds against every other by virtue of being human beings. He opposes these to conditional or hypothetical duties (and rights) which arise from human institutions and compacts. According to this division, property rights clearly fall under the second category. This makes it congruous for Pufendorf to maintain that a person may have a perfect (in the sense of *legally enforceable*) right to her property, which allows her to claim the latter against everyone else and to have it defended by the civil authorities or even by herself, in some very exceptional scenarios. But this perfect and legally enforceable right arises from a human institution, and is subsidiary to the natural right we all have to our basic *suum* and to the things necessary to preserve it. When a person's self-preservation is at stake and the only way to preserve it is by her encroaching upon someone else's property, the legal perfect right of the owner is then restricted by the natural perfect right of the former.

John Salter criticises Pufendorf along similar lines. He says that, contra Grotius, and to avoid the abuse of the stronger over the weaker, Pufendorf founds the right of necessity on the imperfect duty of humanity of the wealthy, but then asserts that, '*in extremis*, the poor can claim the surpluses of the rich "on the same ground as things that are owed by a perfect right"'.[41] Salter takes this to mean that the right to property is conditional upon the performance of the duty of humanity, so that those who refuse to carry out the latter forfeit their otherwise perfect right, which is then transferred to the person in need. For Salter, this renders Pufendorf's account incongruous, and creates two difficulties: it undermines the key distinction between perfect and imperfect duties, and it ends up granting to the poor even stronger rights than Grotius.

Regarding the first difficulty, Salter is right to underline the importance of the distinction between perfect and imperfect duties in Pufendorf's overall theory, as he is to remind us how imperfect duties serve to give the rich the chance to display their kindness freely. As Pufendorf himself says, 'all this merit and obligation is cut off, when we give another, only what he might otherwise, as his own right and due, violently take from us'.[42] But then, Salter objects, 'this is entirely inconsistent with the idea that those who refuse to be charitable should lose their property, as if they are being punished for their refusal to show humanity'.[43]

However, this is not the gist of Pufendorf's argument. In order not to weaken the institution of property—which he thinks is key to keep industriousness, development, security and order—Pufendorf has very good reason to leave the relief of the needy to the goodwill of those who can easily help them out, with no interference or external compulsion under normal circumstances. When humanity has as its object not the mere benefit, but the very survival of others, notwithstanding, it makes sense to make this duty claimable even by force. To be sure, letting people display their solidarity freely is very important for achieving a harmonious society, but it is equally (if not more) important to have in place a principle that protects innocent people from being seriously harmed when this can be done at small cost to others. That the duty of humanity may be enforced is based on this consideration, as well as on the belief that a well-structured institutional system must strive towards the elimination of claims of necessity springing from chronic need.

Salter's second point is that, although Pufendorf criticises Grotius 'for shifting the balance of rights and duties too far in favor of the poor',[44] Pufendorf ends up giving the latter even stronger rights than what Grotius had allowed for. But here Salter takes Pufendorf to be saying something that he doesn't. Pufendorf's complaint against Grotius is not that the latter's argument gives preference to the poor as such, but rather that it leaves the door open for the needy to take from those equally needy, and for the lazy and idle to prey on the hard-working.

It is true, as Salter points out, that the Pufendorfian right of necessity gives the needy the possibility to resort to force against the owners if the latter refuse to aid them, something that Grotius never says or implies. However, as suggested in the previous chapter, such an implication must also be acknowledged by Grotius to make his own account coherent: if the right of necessity is a retreat to the right of common use, then it is not just a privilege but also a claim that may be exercised against those who happen to interfere with the agent's actions when these pertain to the protection of her minimal *suum*.

Summing up, the main point of Swanson's and Salter's criticisms against Pufendorf is that, by letting an otherwise imperfect right to the humanitarian displays of others turn into a perfect, claimable right which may even trump the perfect right to property, he renders his theory incoherent. On the contrary, I have argued that, for Pufendorf, the right of necessity has to be understood as an exception to human laws and as a corollary of natural law. As long as these two different levels are duly distinguished, his theory no longer appears incongruous but, if anything, more attentive to the demands of specific moral contexts.

CONCLUDING REMARKS

In this chapter, I have presented Samuel Pufendorf's account of the right of necessity, founded on the natural pull of self-preservation, and on the idea that the original contracting parties entering into civil society would have included this exceptional clause amidst the standard moral and legal rules.

Against the criticisms that accuse his account of being incongruous, insofar as he upholds both a claimable right of necessity and a perfect right to property, I suggested that the right of necessity for Pufendorf is part of natural law and, consequently, a necessary exception to standard human laws. This means that its recognition does not render property rights incoherent but, on the contrary, it reminds us of one of the primordial functions of this human institution, which is to guarantee a basic level of subsistence for all members of society. The ideal to strive for, tacit in Pufendorf's account, is an institutional system where people only resort to necessity in exceptional, one-off emergencies, rather than on a daily basis because they are chronically deprived.

Three explicit conditions and one implicit condition are then set for the exercise of this right: respectively, the needy agent must restitute whenever possible, he must not take from those equally needy, he must claim this right only as a last resort, and he must not be responsible for his plight. I suggested that these conditions would be demanded by the initial contracting parties designing the agreement to enter civil society, to prevent the potential abuse and/or misuse of this right, while leaving a space for it nonetheless.

On the whole, Pufendorf's account of the right of necessity, ultimately based on the precept of human sociability (which binds us not only to refrain from harming others but also to care for them), is more convincing than Grotius's account of this right as a retreat to the right of common use. While acknowledging the moral importance of individual self-preservation as a basic human drive, Pufendorf emphasises at the same time the key role of minimal solidarity, as manifested in the performance of our common duties of humanity. As will be seen in the coming chapters, these features ought to be revived when giving a contemporary account of the right of necessity.

NOTES

1. This chapter expands on the ideas developed in Alejandra Mancilla, 'Samuel Pufendorf and the Right of Necessity', *Aporia* 3 (2012): 47–64. See Jerome Schneewind, 'Pufendorf's Place in the History of Ethics', *Synthese* 72, 1 (1987); Kari Saastamoinen, 'Pufendorf on Natural Equality, Human Dignity, and Self-Esteem', *Journal of the History of Ideas* 71, 1 (2010); and Stephen Darwall, 'Pufendorf on Morality, Sociability, and Moral Powers', *Journal of the History of Philosophy* 50, 2 (2012).

2. Its abridged version, *The Whole Duty of Man according to the Law of Nature* (1672), was a textbook in universities across Europe, Scotland and the American colonies during the 1700s, earning him a reputation as a major figure in the history of ethics; see Samuel Pufendorf, *The Whole Duty of Man*, ed. Ian Hunter and David Saunders (Indianapolis: Liberty Fund, 2003).

3. 'The alleged law of nature was a law in the sense in which we commonly understand the word "law": it consisted of commands or prohibitions issued by a superior power. But it was presupposed that there already existed a certain order. This natural order was not a law in the sense just mentioned. It was an order based on the fact that human beings have certain qualities that determine their relations to each other, independently of any legislation': Olivecrona, 'Two Levels', 222–23. For a detailed account of Pufendorf's voluntarism, see Schneewind, 'Pufendorf's Place', 148–50, and Jerome Schneewind, *The Invention of Autonomy: A History of Modern Moral Philosophy* (Cambridge: Cambridge University Press, 1998), 118–40.

4. Pufendorf, *DJN* II.III., 14–15, 136–37.
5. Pufendorf, *DJN* I.VII.7, 81.
6. Pufendorf, *DJN* III.I.1, 214.
7. Pufendorf, *DJN* III.III.1, 233.
8. Richard Tuck, *The Rights of War and Peace: Political Thought and the International Order from Grotius to Kant* (Oxford: Oxford University Press, 1999), 152–54 and 165.
9. Pufendorf, *DOH* I.XIII.1, 137.
10. Pufendorf, *DOH* I.V.23, 90.
11. Pufendorf, *DOH* I.V.23, 90.
12. Pufendorf, *DJN* II.IV.1, 154.
13. Buckle, *Natural Law*, 122.
14. Pufendorf, *DJN* III.III.2, 234.
15. Pufendorf, *DJN* III.II.4, 16.
16. Pufendorf, *DJN* II.VI.5, 207.
17. Pufendorf, *DJN* II.VI.5, 207.
18. Pufendorf, *DJN* II.VI.5, 207.
19. Pufendorf, *DJN* II.VI.5, 207.
20. Pufendorf, *DOH*, I.V.23, 90.
21. Pufendorf, *DJN* II.VI.5, 207.
22. Pufendorf, *DJN* II.VI.1, 202.
23. Pufendorf, *DJN* II.VI.2, 203.

24. Pufendorf devotes a whole section of his chapter on the right of necessity to describe what had been considered as standard cases of necessity since ancient times. For example, cutting one's limbs to survive a serious illness; feeding on other men's flesh 'when no other sustenance can be procured'; drawing lots when, in a shipwreck, more people jump into the boat than what the boat can carry; fighting for a wooden plank not to drown in the water; leaving behind soldiers in war in order to save the company; and knocking someone off in a narrow passage to save oneself from a murderer (Pufendorf, *DJN* II.VI.3, 204–5). From then onwards, however, he turns his attention almost exclusively to the right of necessity understood as the right of people in extreme want to take the property of others for their own sustenance.

25. Pufendorf, *DOH* I.II.10, 47. See also Pufendorf, *DJN* I.VI.17, 75.
26. Antonius Matthaeus, *Of Crimes: A Commentary on Books XLVII and XLVIII of the Digest*, ed. M. L. Hewett (Cape Town: Juta, 1987), I.I.7, 49.
27. Matthaeus, *Of Crimes*, I.I.7, 49.
28. Samuel Pufendorf, *Two Books of the Elements of Universal Jurisprudence*, ed. Thomas Behme, trans. William Abbott Oldfather, Natural Law and Enlightenment Classics (Indianapolis: Liberty Fund, 2009), II.VI.6, 239.
29. Pufendorf, *DJN* II.VI.5, 207.
30. Pufendorf, *DJN* II.VI.6, 208–9.
31. Pufendorf, *Two Books* II.IV.7, 331. Pufendorf explicitly condemns those who fail on the performance of their correlative duties due to laziness, lack of trust or plain

maliciousness. Regarding the former, he says that 'the rule of conveniencies and inconveniencies is beside the question, which only supposes some little matter to be taken from a wealthy person, who does not feel the loss, to keep another from perishing by the extremities of hunger or of weather'. Regarding the last two, he claims that 'the law of humanity obliges every man to allow to another the harmless use of his goods or possessions; which upon urgent necessity may be challenged in a forcible manner, inasmuch as the denial of it is presumed to spring, either from groundless diffidence, or from wicked perverseness of mind': Pufendorf, *DJN* II.VI.7, 210, and III.III.5, 238.

32. Pufendorf, *DJN* II.VI.6, 209.
33. Pufendorf, *DJN* II.VI.6, 208.
34. Pufendorf, *The Whole Duty of Man*, I.V.1, 93.
35. Unfortunately, the social connection model of responsibility mentioned in chapter 1 was conceptually unavailable for Pufendorf. This makes his judgments about the moral worthiness of agents a binary matter of guilt or innocence, with no gradations in between.
36. As will be seen in chapter 5, I omit restitution as a condition for the right of necessity to be exercised. When the deprivation is chronic rather than one-off, and when the context is such that potential duty-bearers are co-participants in the same economic order that allows for chronic deprivation to happen, I contend that requiring the needy to compensate those from whom they take would be out of place. If anyone, I suggest that it should be other potential duty-bearers who compensate those who have complied with their immediate and mediate duties of non-interference.
37. Buckle, *Natural Law*, 116.
38. 'The Inconveniences of Servitude' are detailed by Pufendorf in *DJN* VI.III.10, 620–21. See also Buckle, *Natural Law*, 118–24. That determining the moral guilt or innocence of the needy for their plight can easily be done is another questionable assumption made by Pufendorf, that must also be understood against his binary, oversimplified model of moral responsibility.
39. Pufendorf, *DJN* II.VI.6, 208.
40. Swanson, 'The Medieval Foundations', 432.
41. Salter, 'Grotius and Pufendorf', 300.
42. Pufendorf, *DJN* II.VI.6, 208.
43. Salter, 'Grotius and Pufendorf', 301.
44. Salter, 'Grotius and Pufendorf', 301.

Part II

The Right of Necessity and Global Poverty

FOUR
Justifying the Right of Necessity

In this chapter, my aim is to give a normative justification of the right of necessity, understood as the right that someone in need has to take, use and/or occupy the material resources required to secure her self-preservation, even if these resources are someone else's property. Furthermore, my aim is to give a normative justification of the right of necessity that focuses particularly on cases of chronic, rather than one-off need, where this need has been brought about by human-made, structural causes, rather than by natural, unpredictable ones. In particular, I address the question of why this right may be legitimately claimed even if at first sight it seems to go against other important moral rights, such as the right to property.

The short answer to the justification question is that individuals have a right of necessity because they have a right to subsistence, of which the former is a concrete expression—just as self-defence is a concrete expression of the basic right to security. Rather than there being a deep conflict between the postulated right of necessity and property rights, I claim instead that there is continuity, and that the former should be seen as an escape valve, the presence of which is required for any system of property rights to remain morally acceptable.

I proceed as follows. I first clarify what I understand by *subsistence* and offer five arguments in support of the idea that the right to subsistence should be considered as a basic human right. I then argue that, for a system of property rights to be reasonable, the universal fulfilment of the basic right to subsistence must be incorporated into it as an in-built limitation. Next, I show the normative space that the right of necessity should occupy within property systems, as a concrete expression of the right to subsistence. Rather than as clashing with property rights, this moral prerogative ought to be seen as a necessary complement to them in cases where—for either structural or contingent reasons—respect for the former would go against the satisfaction of the individual's basic needs. I conclude by pointing to a gap within the debate on moral cosmopolitanism and global poverty, and by suggesting how embracing the right of necessity of the chronically deprived might help to fill it. Even if not as a final solution, recognition of this right ought to be part of a cosmopolitan morality that purports to respect the basic rights of all and not just some.

THE BASIC RIGHT TO SUBSISTENCE

The basic right to subsistence can be defined as the right to those material provisions required for one's survival or self-preservation; in other words, it is the right to those material provisions required to guarantee a minimal physical and physiological well-being (where the former refers to the body, and the latter to its functions). Air, water, food, shelter, clothing, basic medical provisions, and access to some source of energy constitute the core objects of the basic right to subsistence thus understood.[1]

But why does a bare fact like the physical and physiological interest in subsistence give rise to a normative prescription in the form of a basic right? What is morally so important about subsistence that merits protecting it in this way? That there is such a thing as a basic right to subsistence is one of the four normative assumptions stated at the outset of the book, and here I summarise five arguments in its favour. If one accepts that such a right exists, then one should also accept the right of necessity as its corollary.

A first argument is that subsistence is a necessary condition for having a life and carrying out one's life: if subsistence is not guaranteed, nothing else is. In Henry Shue's words, the right to subsistence is a basic right because without it no other right—basic or not—may be enjoyed. Together with security rights, it is one of those rights upon which all others depend. Basic rights are the moral rock-bottom, 'everyone's minimum reasonable demands upon the rest of humanity ... the rational basis for justified demands the denial of which no self-respecting person can reasonably be expected to accept'.[2] If basic rights are the moral rock bottom, they are so because they reflect every individual's regard for every other individual's fundamental interests in security and survival, equally shared among us all.

A second argument is that a minimum provision of material resources is required by every individual in order to protect her personhood—that is, her status as a normative agent, understood as a core human interest. James Griffin develops this line of thought when he claims that minimum provision (required to maintain one's normative agency) is one of the three constitutive values of personhood or human standing that human rights are supposed to protect, together with autonomy (to develop one's ability to be a normative agent) and liberty (to exercise one's ability to be a normative agent, without undue interference from others).[3] Autonomy rights, liberty rights and the right to a minimum provision are thought to be sufficient to protect normative agency, and to be universal, holding for all human beings everywhere and at all times, and regardless of the existence of institutional arrangements to support them.

A third argument subjects subsistence to a justificatory test and checks whether it meets the criteria to be considered as the object of a basic human right. James Nickel proposes such a test and concludes that it does. He proposes six points. First, inadequate access to subsistence is a major problem and poses a recurrent threat for thousands of human beings. Second, subsistence is such a fundamental human interest that it makes it difficult (if not impossible) to pursue any other interest if it goes unmet. Third, guarantees of access to subsistence are easily translatable into the language of rights as claims, with correlated duties and specified scope and object. Fourth, no weaker norm than a right would be sufficient to protect such an important human interest. Fifth, the burdens imposed by a basic right to subsistence are justifiable; and sixth, it is feasible to implement the right in question.[4]

A fourth way of arguing for a basic right to subsistence is inspired by Alan Gewirth's Principle of Generic Consistency (PGC), whereby every individual must act in accordance with the *generic rights* of her recipients as well as of herself. These generic rights are 'rights to have one's behaviour characterised by the generic features of action and successful action in general: freedom (consisting in control of one's behaviour by one's unforced choice while having knowledge of relevant circumstances) and well-being (consisting in having the general abilities and conditions needed for achieving one's purposes)'.[5] Insofar as it is indispensable to achieve the agent's well-being, the basic right to subsistence of every agent must be respected by every other agent. To do otherwise would be to go against the PGC and, therefore, to contradict oneself.

Finally, that subsistence is the object of a basic right is inspired by the accounts of early modern natural law thinkers such as Grotius and Pufendorf. For them, the negative right not to be unjustly harmed by others (i.e., security), together with the positive right to keep oneself alive (i.e., subsistence), constitute the core of what was known as the *suum*: what belongs to every person—that normative sphere over which every individual is sovereign and upon which others must refrain from encroaching upon. Given its importance, the basic right to subsistence is thus one of those rights that individuals are ultimately permitted to defend by themselves and for themselves—or by someone on their behalf—if their objects are ever endangered.

THE RIGHT TO SUBSISTENCE AS A BUILT-IN LIMIT TO PROPERTY RIGHTS

If one accepts the existence of a basic right to subsistence, one must also grant that any morally acceptable property arrangement must have this right built into it as an internal limitation. In this section I draw from Grotius and Pufendorf to suggest how the right to subsistence is to be incorporated into social contract theories of property. Although they are not the only kind of theories within which a subsistence proviso can be built, I focus on them insofar as one of my initial normative assumptions was presented in social contract terms—namely, that individuals bind themselves to respect property rules to the extent that these rules do not hinder the fulfilment of their basic rights. Demanding otherwise from them would be unreasonable, as it would be irrational for them to accept.[6]

As shown in chapters 2 and 3, for Grotius and Pufendorf the justification of property rights lies on an initial agreement, real or hypothetical, between individuals. What underlies their social contract theories of property rights is the thought that, for that initial agreement to be equitable (or, to put it in the contemporary terminology, reasonable), certain guarantees have to be secured at all times for all parties involved, in exchange for the latter abiding by the established rules. This thought is better understood if one recalls the genealogical story of property rights.

In a state of nature scenario, where no human institutions or compacts are in place, every individual is thought to have a privilege to take and use whatever he needs for his immediate consumption and self-preservation, protected by a basic claim against the interference of others—a claim that he may defend by the use of force if needed.[7] When property rights come into the picture, we can stop worrying about short-term survival. We can start planning ahead, accumulating material things, and living more comfortable lives in general, minimising at the same time the potential for conflict arising amidst a growing population that competes for relatively scarce resources.[8] In a society where property rights have been established, everyone is therefore supposed to be better-off than he was (or would have been) in a state of nature or, at the very least, not worse off. So long as this is true for all members of society, it seems rational for them to respect property rules and to abide by them—and this is what theorists like Grotius and Pufendorf trust will actually happen most of the time.

Put differently, at the foundation of any minimally acceptable system of property rights must lie the following reservation: that, within that system, no one is to fall below the material threshold of well-being required for subsistence.[9] Inversely, no system of property rights may be upheld which does not give this minimal guarantee, so that those whose subsistence rights go unmet have to perish rather than break the rules.

The fact that we are born into societies with already established property rules does not make this reservation any less pressing; on the contrary, it is the very minimum that we may demand if we are to have those rules imposed and enforced upon us.[10] As mentioned before, it is based on this thought that the basic right of subsistence can be conceptualised as an individual immunity, a minimal protection that each deserves as a member of the system.[11]

Having said this, some might fear that making the acceptance of a system of property rules dependent upon the fulfilment of everyone's basic right to subsistence is a daunting requirement for the former. And it could well be if one thinks of the content of such a right as *manna* falling from heaven in large enough quantities over each and every individual. But this is a common misinterpretation of what the right to subsistence means. As Asbjørn Eide explains, based on Henry Shue's typology of duties of avoidance, protection, and aid, first and foremost, '[t]he individual is expected, whenever possible *through his or her own efforts and by the use of his or her resources*, to find ways to ensure the satisfaction of his or her own needs, individually or in association with others'.[12] Use of one's own resources (be they land, capital or labour) assumes of course that the person already has them. This implies that, at the primary level, upholding the right to subsistence consists in respecting the freedom of individuals to engage in those efforts and use of resources. At a secondary level, individual freedom of action must be protected, setting the limits against other agents through rules that impede unfair competition and fraud, facilitate contracts, promote ethical behaviour in trade, and so on and so forth. Presumably, this duty ought also to include protecting against asymmetric power relations that contracting parties might otherwise be placed in.[13] It is only at a tertiary level that the obligation to directly fulfil the right to subsistence kicks in, for example, when states have to provide employment opportunities or direct material assistance to those who cannot procure them by themselves or from others.

The underlying assumption, then, must be that the vast majority of individuals will do well (or, at least, not worse than in a state of nature scenario) in a society where property rules are in place. And they will do well not because the things they need are going to be handed in directly to them while they wait passively, but because opportunities and resources are going to be available for them to pursue their living through their own efforts.[14] For those who are not in a position to do this (because they are too young, too old, too sick, or because their rights were not respected or protected in the first place), there must be provisions to secure their subsistence, through the assistance of other individuals, organisations or the state itself. Incorporating the right to be given minimal provisions if one is not able to secure one's subsistence through one's own means is not a difficult task for social contract theories. In Rawlsian fashion, if one imagines oneself in the position of the contracting parties, who agree on the initial principles of justice without knowing what place those who they represent will later occupy in society, it makes sense to include it.[15] Alternatively, if one follows Grotius's and Pufendorf's story, then one must presume that—for the sake of equity—the original legislators would have left this provision in place. A different strategy is to appeal to the conjunction of two of the initial normative assumptions proposed at the beginning of this book: if one endorses the first tenet of moral cosmopolitanism (namely, that individuals are the ultimate unit of moral concern), and one believes that individuals have a basic right to subsistence, then it follows that this right ought to be fulfiled on behalf of those who cannot do it by themselves.

THE RIGHT OF NECESSITY AS A CONCRETE EXPRESSION OF THE BASIC RIGHT TO SUBSISTENCE

In the previous section, I suggested why a subsistence proviso must be incorporated into a system of property rights for the latter to be morally acceptable, and showed how this may be justified within social contract theories.

No matter how well thought-out a system of property is, however, there is always the possibility that some individual will fall below the subsistence threshold, and that his only means of survival will be to except himself from the rules. No matter how fair the rules we set, in other words, there will always be contingent circumstances where following them would go against the basic purpose that they were designed to attain. This is where the right of necessity enters into the normative picture—namely, as a concrete expression of the right to subsistence when no other means are available, and when respect for the rules would endanger rather than protect one's self-preservation.

Imagine a society, *Overland*, where property rules function to the benefit of all its members and where there are various mechanisms in place to secure the bare essentials (and maybe even more) to those who cannot provide those goods by themselves. In Overland, people are quite sporty and love being outdoors. But no place is perfect, and Overland's weather is unpredictable. Lonely hikers sometimes get caught inadvertently in the middle of mountain storms. Luckily, Overlanders also love keeping huts in the mountains, and this allows hikers in a plight to break into whoever's hut they find to seek refuge and maybe also prepare some food while the storm lasts. On the understanding that such an emergency may happen to anyone, Overlanders have left this individual prerogative to break into huts and eat other people's food as a legitimate limitation to their standard property rules.[16] Having reflected on the issue, Overlanders know that not doing so would be inequitable, in the sense of overly taxing for those who happen to fall in such need. Plus, these situations occur only exceptionally and do not constitute a major burden for the hut owners, who are moreover offered compensation for the damages after the emergency has passed.

Ideally, the exercise of the right of necessity by particular individuals within a given society should be restricted to hiker-in-the-storm kind of scenarios and not much else. Given the potentially unsettling effects that the frequent exercise of such a prerogative would have, property rules should therefore be set in such a way that the resulting system resembles Overland as much as possible—that is, it should be a system where the basic right to subsistence of all persons under normal circumstances is secured.[17] But what happens if this is not the case? What happens if people fall in dire need and there are no provisions in place for them, so that their choice is either to respect the rules and thence endanger their subsistence or to break the rules and take other people's property in order to get out of their plight?

Imagine now a different society, *Underland*, where property rules are heavily enforced, even though they have not been especially well designed to meet the basic needs of all Underlanders. If in need, sometimes the latter are lucky enough to get help from some good-willed individual or some charitable organisation, but sometimes they do not, and the institutional system fails to provide even the minimal material provisions for them. If they dare to ignore property rules to get what they need, Underlanders end up being punished by society and by the law—if not plainly harmed or even killed by the owners in so-called *legitimate self-defence*, which the authorities are willing to back up. Like in Overland, in Underland trespasses on other people's property are allowed only in contingent situations like the hiker-in-the-storm scenario. But, unlike in Overland, in Underland there is a group of chronically deprived people who have nothing to resort to when their very subsistence is threatened.

In our current world, acceptance of the right of necessity remains confined to cases of one-off, mostly naturally caused emergencies, as though we already lived in Overland, even if we don't. This means that if an individual takes someone else's property and claims that he did so because his right to subsistence was unmet, he will probably end up punished by society and by the law: common morality tends to sanction property infringements almost with no exceptions, and legal systems reject exculpation based on extreme poverty or indigence.[18] My contention, on the contrary, is that it is unreasonable and ultimately unacceptable to impose a narrow conception of the right of necessity when the global economic order (and, within it, the framing of property rights) has not been designed in a way that secures access to minimum material provisions for all individuals, and involves processes which result in the basic right to subsistence of many to remain chronically unmet. Under such a system, the right of necessity ought to be allowed as a moral prerogative of the individual, a last resort for those who have no other means to survive. This claim, then, relies on the empirical assumption that there is one global economic society, increasingly interconnected and increasingly interdependent, within which members hold certain minimal rights against, and bear minimal duties to, each other.

A GAP WITHIN MORAL COSMOPOLITANISM, AND HOW TO FILL IT

I have said so far that, if we accept that the basic right to subsistence constitutes a built-in limitation to any reasonable theory of property rights, we should also be ready to grant a right of necessity to those whose basic needs within society go unmet, regardless of whether this is due to contingent or to structural reasons. In a society that provides universal access to those material resources required for self-preservation, the exercise of this moral prerogative would be in fact exceptional, and limited to one-off, urgent situations. In a society where this is not the case, contrariwise, the exercise of the right of necessity by the chronically deprived ought to be allowed, if not as the best solution, as the least one should grant if one wishes to recognise their basic right to subsistence.

With this in mind, it is surprising that, in the abundant literature on moral cosmopolitanism and global poverty, recognition of the right of necessity of the chronically deprived is rare.[19] As stated at the outset of the book, most of the contemporary discussion on this topic—even when starting from a human rights discourse—has so far been conducted in terms of what the haves must do for, or stop doing to, the have-nots.

Thomas Pogge, one of the main proponents of the global justice approach, is a clear representative of this drift. Pogge describes his view as putting the emphasis on 'how well the global institutional order is doing, compared to its feasible and reachable alternatives, in regard to the fundamental human interests that matter from a moral point of view'.[20] These fundamental interests are best described in the language of human rights: 'A commitment to human rights involves one in recognizing that human persons with a past or potential future ability to engage in moral conversation and practice have certain basic needs, and that these needs give rise to weighty moral demands. The object of each of these basic human needs is the object of a human right'.[21]

Starting from the Rawlsian conception of justice as the first virtue of human institutions, Pogge then focuses on the causal and moral analysis of global institutional schemes (like trade barriers, international agreements and what he calls the *resource privilege* and *borrowing privilege* of governments), to the extent that these can further or hinder the realisation of these rights.[22] Pogge's claim is that having a clear picture of the ways in which the institutional design affects the fulfilment of human rights globally is necessary for moral agents to come to realise their duties in this respect. These are 'institutional negative duties correlative to human rights'.[23] They are institutional, as opposed to interactional, because they are not first-order principles regulating the relationship between individuals or groups directly, but rather second-order principles assessing the conduct of agents with respect to institutional schemes, which in turn regulate the conduct between agents.[24] And they are negative, as opposed to positive, because they are duties to ensure that one's conduct does not unduly harm others—in this case, by participating in the design or upholding of a coercive institutional order that foreseeably and avoidably deprives others of the objects of their human rights.

Pogge's definition of *harm*; his conception of duties correlative to human rights in institutional, rather than interactional, terms; and his empirical assumptions (especially that the global order in fact engenders and reproduces global poverty) have been extensively scrutinised.[25] Little attention has been paid, in comparison, to the full implications of his conception of human rights.[26] Pogge himself, in fact, does not explicitly state these implications.

Pogge says that human rights are direct moral claims against any coercive social institutions imposed upon oneself, insofar as they can enable or hinder our access to the objects of those rights. By extension, human rights are also indirect moral claims against anyone involved in the design or imposition of such institutions. Depending on how widely we define this involvement, human rights can be understood as indirect claims of every individual against each and every other individual who participates to some extent in these arrangements. Compared to his meticulous analysis and justification of negative institutional duties to fulfil human rights, Pogge does not consider in much depth the question of what actions pending moral claims entitle their holders to undertake. In fact, he does so only in passing, when he says that 'a valid *complaint* against our social institutions can be presented by all those whose physical integrity is not sufficiently secure', and admits that 'human rights ultimately make *demands* upon (especially the more influential) citizens [of one's society]'.[27]

The fact that Pogge does not dwell on what these demands and complaints actually amount to is curious, especially given his sombre picture of the current global state of affairs. According to his own estimations, '360 million human beings have died prematurely from poverty-related causes, with some 18 million more added each year'.[28] Coupled with the assumption that the coercive global order is avoidably and foreseeably bringing about these grim statistics, because those who ought to are failing to perform their negative institutional duties, this should raise an obvious question: May the needy do no more than *complain* and *demand* while their human rights are being systematically unfulfiled and violated? Or is this not an extremely tepid recommendation considering the gravity of what is at stake?

To these questions, Pogge might reply along the lines developed by Onora O'Neill in the course of her meticulous criticism of the language of welfare rights—more specifically, subsistence rights—and her defence of the language of obligations instead. In short, O'Neill's thought is that rights are claims—that is, they have attached to them corollary obligations. In the case of liberty rights, the problem of allocating the latter is easily solved, insofar as these are rights against all other individuals and all other institutions (that allocation of first-order obligations is straightforward does not solve, of course, the different and equally important matter of how to assign second-order obligations to ensure that liberty rights are respected, protected, and fulfiled). Contrariwise, because welfare rights are claims to certain goods and services, we cannot know who violates them unless we have already specified who has the correlated obligation to ensure that these goods and services are provided. Insofar as these obligations remain unallocated—that is, insofar as we remain in the situation that we are today at the global level—'a so-called right to food, as many other "rights" that would be important for the needy, will be only manifesto rights'.[29]

O'Neill thus characterises welfare rights discourse as passive and recipient-directed: 'It is a matter of thinking about what one ought to get or to have done for one, and about what others (but which others?) ought to do or provide for one'; '[i]f there are to be rights to goods or services, those goods and services must be provided, and more specifically provided by someone'; 'those who claim still see themselves within an overall framework of recipience. They still demand that others act rather than they do so themselves'.[30] The language of obligations, on the other hand, is characterised as action-guiding and concerned with what ought to be done. On this basis, she concludes, the latter and not the former should be the preferred normative starting point when tackling issues like global poverty and insecure access to the objects of the basic right to subsistence.

While I am sympathetic to O'Neill's analysis, I disagree with her characterisation of the language of rights as recipient-oriented. Moreover, I suggest that the solution she points to (where obligations occupy the main normative space) should be supplemented by bringing into the picture the right of necessity and its implications.

To start with the characterisation of the language of rights as recipient-oriented, although this is not a project of social epistemology, the assumption that something like the basic right to subsistence may be realised only in certain ways (which seem to be those acceptable for the non-needy majority in Western societies), and not others (which might be those more realistically accessible for the needy), can well be interpreted as what Miranda Fricker has called a *hermeneutical injustice*. Hermeneutical injustices take place when 'a gap in collective interpretive resources puts someone at an unfair disadvantage when it comes to making sense of their social experiences'.[31] In the case under discussion, by constraining what *claiming* a basic right involves to speech acts like *insisting, demanding, entreating, pleading, complaining, objecting to, proposing*, and so on and so forth, the possibility that the fulfilment of the right to subsistence may come through direct physical action, like *taking, using, consuming* and *occupying* things and places, seems to be precluded. That is, there is a language gap that does not allow those whose right to subsistence remains unfulfiled to conceptualise their right in ways different from those standardly prescribed. Furthermore, insofar as they choose to act in ways that do not fall under the umbrella of acceptable ways of *claiming*, they run the risk of being socially marginalised and criminally prosecuted. Critics who have questioned the language switch from the *Rights of Man* to *human rights* in contemporary political philosophy and politics make a similar observation: while the former embody the original raison d'être of rights (i.e., individual moral powers to act in the world), the latter risk becoming watered-down versions of the former, never to be realised by their holders, but always by others (not necessarily appointed by them) on their behalf.[32] If welfare rights and, specifically, the basic right to subsistence invoke an image of passivity, this connection is thus not one that the needy choose to create, but one imposed (deliberately or not) by those who would prefer the latter to constrain their actions in this way. But it suffices to look at the history of rights to realise that this connection is quite a recent one, and one that would have astonished both those who initially theorised about these rights and those who fought for enacting them.[33]

Furthermore, I suggest that, by bringing the right of necessity into O'Neill's analysis, the normative landscape so far presented changes quite dramatically. If one understands the right to subsistence as a basic moral right, and if one also accepts that the right of necessity is a concrete expression of it, then the problem of allocating immediate duties is at least partly solved by the right-holder herself, or by someone acting on her behalf. By taking, using and/or occupying the property of others, the agent straightway singles out specific duty-bearers—individual or collective, institutional or not. Just like Samaritan duties, which arise by virtue of the immediate moral relationship established between someone in need of aid and someone able to provide it, the immediate duty correlated to the right of necessity arises by virtue of the situation in which the needy individual comes across someone else's property, which she needs for her self-preservation.

To be sure, the problem of allocation is *partly*, rather than *fully* solved, insofar as there are millions today who are in a morally legitimate position to exercise their right, but who are at the same time practically incapacitated from so doing. That this is the case should lead O'Neill, Pogge and the whole host of cosmopolitan theorists to remap the normative landscape of global poverty accordingly. Among other things, they should start to pay attention to actual ways in which real, needy people exercise their right on a daily basis and get punished for so doing; to inquire into other, potential ways in which the latter may exercise their right, or ask others to exercise it on their behalf; to use the right of necessity as a normative cornerstone from which other rights of the needy—paradigmatically, the right of collective resistance—may be justified; and to reconceptualise the final duty to put an end to chronic deprivation globally in the following terms: to wit, as a duty not to create and/or uphold conditions under which people who may claim necessity (because chronically deprived) are actually prevented from doing it, or, positively stated, a duty to create conditions under which the legitimate exercise of the right of necessity by the chronically deprived simply disappears.

CONCLUDING REMARKS

Because of its paramount moral importance, the satisfaction of the basic right to subsistence may be pursued by the individual even if this ultimately implies encroaching upon the property of third parties. This is the normative space that I have defended for the right of necessity in this chapter.

In a society that respects and protects the basic right to subsistence of all its members, and provides for those who cannot through their own efforts get what they need, the right of necessity does not entirely disappear, but is left as an exceptional moral prerogative limited to hiker-in-the-storm-like scenarios. On the contrary, in a society where the basic right to subsistence of many remains unmet due to some structural deficiency, it is unreasonable to demand that those deprived endanger their very self-preservation for the sake of respecting the rules. Letting them exercise their right is the minimum that one should grant for those who have no other means to resort to.

I have suggested, moreover, that contemporary moral cosmopolitan discourses around global poverty have tended to obscure or plainly ignore this fundamental feature of the basic right to subsistence—namely, that it may be ultimately claimed by the individual himself, where *claiming* does not mean *petitioning, entreating, complaining* or *pleading* but directly *taking, using* and/or *occupying* the resources needed, even if these are the property of others. To leave a normative space for the right of necessity as a concrete expression of the basic right to subsistence is to bring back what those who initially theorised about rights thought them to be: moral sanctions, prerogatives for individual action, permissions to act that each person was entitled to in order to be and to remain sovereign over her own sphere. Undoubtedly, theorists in the past, like theorists today, foresaw the radical implications of rights theories for the ordering and structuring of society. The point of recognising that individuals never relinquish their basic rights, notwithstanding, is not to promote a return (or descent) to a state of nature setting, where individuals hold and defend these rights with their own hands. Rather, it is to serve as an urgent reminder that the basis over which society has to be constructed must have these rights as starting points and built-in limitations throughout.

NOTES

1. For the purposes of this discussion I limit the objects of the right to subsistence to those indispensable to attain a minimally tolerable quality of life. It is thus a much more modest interpretation than the one proposed, for example, in Article 25 of the Universal Declaration of Human Rights: 'Everyone has the right to a standard of living adequate for the health and well-being of himself and his family, including food, clothing, housing, medical care and necessary social services, and the right to security in the event of unemployment, sickness, disability, widowhood, old age or other lack of livelihood in circumstances beyond his control': United Nations, Universal Declaration of Human Rights, accessed January 12, 2016, http://www.un.org/en/universal-declaration-human-rights/. As explained in chapter 1, this is not to say that this minimalistic reading is the only defensible one, but only that other arguments that I do not offer here would have to be developed to justify more ambitious versions of the basic right to subsistence and, therefore, of the right of necessity as its concrete expression.

2. Shue, *Basic Rights*, 19.

3. James Griffin, *On Human Rights* (Oxford: Oxford University Press, 2008), 33ff. Although Griffin describes his approach as *trinist*, that is as grounding human rights on three distinct values, I agree with John Tasioulas that this account is better described as *dualist*, insofar as minimum provision is a condition for the realisation of the values of autonomy and liberty: John Tasioulas, 'Taking Rights out of Human Rights', in *Griffin on Human Rights*, ed. Roger Crisp (Oxford: Oxford University Press, 2014), 22.

4. James Nickel, *Making Sense of Human Rights*, 2nd ed. (Malden, MA: Blackwell Publishing, 2007), 145–52.

5. Alan Gewirth, 'The Justification of Morality', *Philosophical Studies* 53, 2 (1988): 245.

6. Lockean theories that conceptualise property rights as natural (as opposed to conventional) must also incorporate a subsistence proviso to remain coherent. See Gillian Brock's persuasive argument of why Robert Nozick's libertarianism must include such a clause: Gillian Brock, 'Is Redistribution to Help the Needy Unjust?', *Analysis* 55, 1 (1995). I leave out three types of theories of property rights that, however influential, seem unreasonable when it comes to the question of why each individual who partakes in the system ought to follow its rules if the latter happen to threaten her own survival. The first are Humean theories, which take the rules of justice—and, within them, the rules of property—to consist in whatever was decided on at a certain point in time to settle conflict, without necessarily providing any guarantees for those in a weaker position within society (for discussion, see Jeremy Waldron, 'The Advantages and Difficulties of the Humean Theory of Property', *Social Philosophy and Policy* 11 [1994]). The second are consequentialist theories that justify upholding property rules so long as the benefits for the better-off outweigh the costs for the worse-off. There are two main problems with these theories. The first is their reliance on the controversial assumption that the worse-off are in fact not any worse than they would have been without any property arrangements. The second is that what count as *benefits* and *costs* are usually determined by the propertied and not by the propertyless (see, for example, the reasoning of the English Court of Appeal in *London Borough*

of Southwark v. Williams, ch. 1, n. 49). The third kind of theory that I leave out are hardline libertarian theories with no provisos on appropriation, or with provisos that do not take into account the satisfaction of even the basic needs of others. Here comes to mind Jan Narveson's idea that first possessors have a right to what they possess, while latecomers 'must negotiate further uses of what is already owned': Jan Narveson, 'Property and Rights', *Social Philosophy and Policy* 27, 1 (2010): 134.

7. As explained in more detail in chapters 2 and 3, this is implicit in Grotius's account, and clearly explicit in Pufendorf's. Their version of the state of nature, to recall, is not rightless.

8. I say *relatively scarce,* because they are, however, enough to provide for all.

9. Note that this works against the assumption, tacit in both Grotius and Pufendorf, that nature is plentiful enough to provide at least the basics for subsistence to everyone under normal circumstances.

10. For a similar view, see Gerhard Øverland's *adjustment principle*: 'In ordering the institutional scheme the aim should be to minimize the likelihood that a person finds himself in a situation in which we would not think it wrong of him if he deliberately breaks the law to obtain particular material goods': Gerhard Øverland, 'Just Adjustments', in *Treating Others* (Oslo: Unipub, 2002), 153. Øverland's proposal differs from mine, however, in two important respects. First, it makes what may be minimally demanded from the system wholly contingent upon how wealthy the latter is, without setting a lower threshold. Second, it suggests that, if the adjustment principle is not met, it is equally plausible to change either the economic order (and, presumably, the property laws within it, as I have been suggesting) or the criminal law. That is, Øverland seems to concede that we may keep an economic order that does not guarantee that the adjustment principle will be met, so long as we do not punish those who break the law to obtain the required material goods. For the moral dilemma created by this second option, see Victor Tadros, 'Poverty and Criminal Responsibility', *Journal of Value Inquiry* 43 (2009).

11. Here liberal-minded social contract theorists might object that these theories must not necessarily include this clause. Coercion, even coercion that costs lives, is of the essence of any political system. In the case of liberalism, the argument is generally the following: no one is singled out for killing, but everyone undertakes risks voluntarily—for example, by driving on highways, and getting vaccinated. The increase in quality of life and life expectancy are so great for the vast majority that they justify imposing these risks on everyone. Accordingly, since the unilateral enforcement of the right of necessity by the chronically deprived would threaten the very system that brings most people out of poverty, it should not be allowed. The problem with this objection is that it treats as similar two very different kinds of situations with two very different associated costs: by driving or getting vaccinated, I make a gamble, so to speak, based on the low probability that I will get harmed or even killed by using these services, against the high probability that I will reap a lot of benefit from them. To put it more dramatically, if I become a martyr, I am the martyr of my own cause. When I am chronically deprived within a given society and I am prohibited from unilaterally enforcing my right of necessity, on the contrary, I am not undertaking any risk on the expectation that it will be for my own benefit. Rather, my position is that of a martyr of society's cause. That no one may be required to be a martyr of society's cause is another way to put the claim I am making. I thank Avery Kolers for pressing me to clarify this point.

12. Asbjørn Eide, 'Article 25', in *The Universal Declaration of Human Rights: A Commentary,* ed. Asbjørn Eide and T. Swinehart (Oslo: Scandinavian University Press, 1993), 387; emphasis added.

13. I thank Michael Neu for suggesting this addition.

14. There is a further, optimistic assumption that people will be able to do this without exploiting or being exploited by others. In chapter 5, I address the question whether exploitative jobs should be considered as an available option before resorting to the exercise of the right of necessity.

15. Eventually, Rawls did include such a principle as lexically prior to his two principles of justice: 'In particular, the first principle covering the equal basic rights and liberties may easily be preceded by a lexically prior principle requiring that citizens' basic needs be met, at least insofar as their being met is necessary for citizens to understand and to be able fruitfully to exercise those rights and liberties. Certainly any such principle must be assumed in applying the first principle': John Rawls, *Political Liberalism*, expanded ed. (New York: Columbia University Press, 2005), 7.

16. Presumably, Overlanders have also left a space for the exercise of that individual prerogative in other situations where following the standard procedures would hinder rather than promote the ends for which those procedures were put in place. For example, taking someone else's car to bring a seriously injured person to the hospital, using and maybe even wrecking someone else's lifeboat to save someone from drowning, and so on.

17. Recall that the underlying assumption is that there are enough material resources available, and that access to them and distribution of them is feasible.

18. For an explanation of why indigence is not a legally acceptable basis for exculpation, see Waldron, 'Why Indigence Is Not a Justification'.

19. Among the exceptions, Henry Shue acknowledges that if the principles of justice of a certain society do not guarantee the fulfilment of the basic right to subsistence, an alternative is 'to reserve to oneself the option of taking by stealth or force, if necessary, one's vital necessities'. Doing so may be no more rational than respecting those institutions and dying out of neglect as a result, Shue concedes, but 'it is not clearly less rational' either: Shue, *Basic Rights*, 128. Alan Gewirth adopts a similar position when he asks, more generally, 'How can the moral necessity of human rights be upheld in the face of the wrongful contingencies, the rights-violations, of the actual world?', and answers that '[t]he use of force or power is not at all precluded by the status of human rights as highly valuable norms for action. Human rights need not be empirically ineffectual; on the contrary, it is permissible to threaten or actually to use force in order to advance what is morally justified. To be sure, the use of force should not make things worse for the victims of rights-violations; but this is a matter of empirical calculation, not of moral prohibition': Alan Gewirth, 'Duties to Fulfill the Human Rights of the Poor', in *Freedom from Poverty as a Human Right*, ed. Thomas Pogge (New York: Oxford University Press, 2007), 226–27. Although they leave the door open for individuals to claim the objects of this right by themselves if that is the only means to secure their subsistence, neither Shue nor Gewirth develop this idea and its implications further, which is unfortunate.

20. Pogge, *Politics as Usual*, 24.
21. Pogge, *World Poverty and Human Rights*, 64.
22. See Pogge, *World Poverty and Human Rights*, 159–72.
23. Pogge, *Politics as Usual*, 30.
24. Pogge, *World Poverty and Human Rights*, 176–77.
25. On Pogge's unduly stretched notion of harm, see Christian Barry and Gerhard Øverland, 'The Feasible Alternatives Thesis: Kicking Away the Livelihoods of the Global Poor?', *Politics Philosophy Economics* 11, 1 (2012). See also Patten, 'Should We Stop Thinking about Poverty in Terms of Helping the Poor?'; Matthias Risse, 'Do We Owe the Global Poor Assistance or Rectification?'; and Debra Satz, 'What Do We Owe the Global Poor?'—all three in *Ethics and International Affairs* 19, 1 (2005). On the charge that Pogge fails to appreciate the relation between interactional and institutional duties, see Carol C. Gould, 'Coercion, Care, and Corporations: Omissions and Commissions in Thomas Pogge's Political Philosophy', *Journal of Global Ethics* 3, 3 (2007). On Pogge's controversial empirical assumptions, see Joshua Cohen, 'Philosophy, Social Science and Poverty', in *Thomas Pogge and His Critics*, ed. Alison Jaggar (Malden, MA: Polity Press, 2010).

26. An exception is Lippert-Rasmussen, 'Global Injustice and Redistributive Wars'.
27. Pogge, *World Poverty*, 53, 70; emphasis added. A similar language is used by Elizabeth Ashford, who affirms that '[e]ach person is entitled to the objects of their

human rights and can *justifiably* insist on them as their due'. When these rights are unmet, individuals 'could justifiably *complain* that they were being deprived of what they were entitled to as a matter of basic justice', and, when these deprivations become chronic, the individual 'can *object to* a set of principles under which his or her being secured access to basic necessities is treated as morally optional, and can *propose* an alternative set of principles under which it is considered to be an enforceable duty of justice': Elizabeth Ashford, 'Duties Imposed by the Human Right to Basic Necessities', in *Freedom from Poverty as a Human Right*, ed. Thomas Pogge (Oxford: Oxford University Press, 2007), 185ff.; emphasis added. This image of the needy sitting down at the bargaining table to persuade those who impose the rules on them seems to me overly optimistic, not to say disingenuous.

28. Pogge, *Politics as Usual*, 50.

29. O'Neill, 'Rights, Obligations and Needs', 98.

30. Onora O'Neill, *Bounds of Justice* (Cambridge: Cambridge University Press, 2000), 100; Onora O'Neill, 'The Dark Side of Human Rights', *International Affairs* 81, 2 (2005): 427–28; and O'Neill, 'Rights, Obligations and Needs', 97.

31. Miranda Fricker, *Epistemic Injustice: Power and the Ethics of Knowing* (Oxford: Oxford University Press, 2007), 1.

32. This is not the place to offer a summary of the abundant bibliography in critical theory and social sciences devoted to the critique of contemporary human rights language, especially of how it subjects the needy to being quiet. But see, for example, Jacques Rancière, 'Who Is the Subject of the Rights of Man?', in *Dissensus: On Politics and Aesthetics* (London: Bloomsbury, 2010), 80ff.

33. That the term *welfare right* is a relatively new one does not mean that the concept of welfare rights did not exist before. As already shown, the idea that the interest in self-preservation grounds an individual right to self-preservation has a long philosophical pedigree.

FIVE
Content, Form and Conditions

In this chapter, I refer in more detail to the content of the right of necessity—that is, what the right of necessity is a right to. I then refer to its form, which I take to be that of a *liberty*, understood as a *privilege* plus a *claim of non-interference* against others. Next, I expound three necessary and jointly sufficient conditions for the exercise of this right and anticipate some central objections to the account presented.

THE CONTENT OF THE RIGHT OF NECESSITY

As a concrete expression of the basic right to subsistence, the right of necessity is a right to those material provisions required for one's self-preservation, or to the means required to obtain them. It is, then, a right to those things that one directly needs to keep oneself alive (air, water, food, elements for basic healthcare, and protection from the elements in the form of clothing, shelter and energy), or to whatever indirectly serves to obtain the former.[1]

I mentioned previously that I opt for a minimalistic conception of *subsistence*, where the latter is limited to those aspects of our physical and physiological well-being that we share with other animals. These set an absolute threshold, because they regard those elements that human beings anywhere at any time need to stay alive.

Thus far my account concurs with the traditional accounts of the right of necessity given by authors like Aquinas, Grotius and Pufendorf, whose examples focus on needy individuals taking things directly used for self-preservation, most commonly food. In addition to this, however, I propose to include as legitimate objects of the right of necessity something that in the traditional versions is omitted—namely, those things that may indirectly serve to obtain the former. The content of the right of necessity, therefore, includes the content of the basic right to subsistence but is not limited to it. In this way, it covers situations where the person in need might not be able to find the resources required directly but might be able to find the means to then access them. For example, while in a rural area it might be straightforward to find food and water for direct consumption, in an urban setting it might be necessary to get money to then go and pay for them.

Some might object here that, by considering as legitimate targets of appropriation not only the means of subsistence but also any means to those means, the content of the right of necessity could become so inflated as to include anything from diamonds to be exchanged for materials to build a shelter, to nuclear warheads to be used as leverage in negotiating some food, or even human hostages used to get money to then go and buy provisions for one's family.[2] This objection regards the *kind of things* that may count as legitimate means to the means of subsistence.

I suggest that the answer has to do with the *kind of need* that the right of necessity addresses. In previous chapters, I expounded why it seems morally appropriate to understand the right of necessity in a broad rather than in a narrow sense—that is, why it should be accepted not only as an escape valve for those who are in the middle of one-off, unexpected emergencies but also for those in a state of continued deprivation. I claimed that this was not an original idea, but one developed mainly from Pufendorf's account of why the right of necessity must be accepted within a society that has not yet secured some minimum material provisions for everyone. I further suggested that, given the interconnectedness of the current world economic order, this principle ought to be applied globally rather than only domestically. What Pufendorf leaves undeveloped, however, is the answer to the question of what the needy person may legitimately take as a means to get out of her plight. To fill that gap, my suggestion is that what should count as legitimate means are *at least* those things required to secure one's immediate subsistence, as well as (depending on the circumstances, as will be explained below) those things required to sustain the person indefinitely rather than only fleetingly. If what the person is trying to solve is her permanent state of deprivation and she has no good reason to believe that she will exit that state any time soon, then taking, using and/or occupying those things required for her subsistence on a more permanent basis seems a better and more efficient strategy than taking those things that will cover her subsistence needs only momentarily. In the case of landless peasants, for example, it seems better to claim one's right of necessity to get a piece of land to become self-sustaining, rather than to jump the neighbour's fence every day in order to take some vegetables for dinner. In the case of the urban homeless, it seems better to occupy an empty patch permanently rather than move around trying to find a different shelter every night. To put it in one phrase, taking someone else's fishing net once seems like a better and more efficient course of action overall than taking someone else's catch day after day.

However, this might turn out to be overdemanding for those whose property is being targeted. As individual duty-bearers, the least one should do for others who are in a plight is to let them take what they need to secure their immediate subsistence. The plausibility of the original account of the right of necessity relies on this idea, and it is important to keep it. On the same grounds, it seems too much to require individual duty-bearers to let the needy take things centrally related to their life-projects, because the needy find them suitable to guarantee their subsistence in the middle and long-term. This does not preclude the possibility that the needy request these things and that the owners of the resources consent to give them away. But this is one step further from what the right of necessity here presented requires the duty-bearers to do, and in what follows I do not give arguments to support this kind of takings. All along, it must be borne in mind that I am assuming that the duty-bearers have no clear-cut, direct responsibility for the plight of the needy, but are rather co-participants in a complex institutional mesh where responsibilities are dispersed and very difficult—if not impossible—to determine in a precise way. That is why I suggested, in chapter 1, conceptualising the kind of normative relationships arising from such a context along the lines of Iris Marion Young's social connection model of responsibility. If it were possible to establish clear-cut, direct responsibilities of certain agents (individual or collective) in the plight of the needy, then the former would be *liable*, and the latter's claim of necessity would be compounded with an equally direct claim of justice, presumably much more demanding. To be sure, between direct and diffuse responsibility there are many other shades depending, for instance, on the agents' awareness (or culpable ignorance) of their contribution to processes that create and/or uphold structural injustice; their capability (but failure) to act otherwise; their degree of involvement in the institutional shaping and framing that affects the needy, and so on and so forth. Building a thorough taxonomy of the different ways in which claims of necessity and claims of justice should be compounded according to different factors such as these would lead this project, however, in a different direction. For current purposes, then, I assume—unless stated otherwise—that potential claimants have no particular grievances against potential duty-bearers, but they are rather loose co-participants in one global economic order.

Having said this, there is a distinction to be made between the taking of things that are productively used and/or occupied by the owners, and which are related to their life-plans in a central way, and those that are not.[3] On the one hand, it seems clear that the needy person ought to request the owner's authorisation if what she is intending to do is to work part of the land that the owner uses, or squat in his backyard on a long-term basis, or take his fishing boat for good. On the other hand, if the needy person occupies a derelict patch of land or an empty building owned by someone who neither uses it nor occupies it nor needs it in any central way to pursue her life-projects, she may go ahead. In a social context where there are some who struggle to find a shelter, while at the same time there is an abundance of unused, unproductive housing resources, the permissibility of this kind of takings seems plausible. I suggest that this is because, in cases of this kind, by thus acting the needy are not merely satisfying their immediate need, but they are also helping to rectify an unfair *general* state of affairs (which is different from the claim that the needy have a *particular* claim of justice against the owners). This point is especially relevant in many countries today, where the scarcity of housing alternatives for the worse-off contrasts with the abundance of super expensive properties owned as assets for rental. That there is a growing acceptance of squatters' rights in this context was recently confirmed by *Podemos*, a popular political party in Spain, which proposed to expropriate all empty houses and legalise their occupation. Supporting this motion, some Spanish judges chose to absolve squatters instead of criminalising them.[4]

Regarding morally problematic means, such as the taking of hostages or the use of nuclear weapons as a leverage to obtain something in exchange, I am suspicious of these examples insofar as they evoke an image of the right of necessity holder as a violent *other* that is to be feared rather than respected. Notwithstanding, let me say something on each of them separately. In the case of hostages, it is not the person's external property but the person herself who becomes the object of the right. She is expected to let others use not only her material belongings without interference but also herself. In Kantian terms, the person here is used merely as a means to an end. Given that complying with such a duty would compromise her individual liberty (which is an equally basic human interest and, therefore, an equally important source of rights), I contend that no one has a duty to be held as a hostage so that others may satisfy their basic needs. As will be explained next, if the cost of someone exercising her right of necessity is that someone else will have her basic liberties violated, then such a right does not hold—or, if it does, it amounts to a mere privilege, the exercise of which the latter may or may not grant. For the right of necessity to generate correlated duties, the potential duty-bearer must be able to exercise a minimal solidarity towards the right-holder without it coming at such a high cost that it undermines other equally important moral values and interests—in this case, her own personal freedom. Again, it is important to keep this separate from the question of what the needy may do to others when these others have been directly involved in disadvantaging them. As already said, in the latter case their claim of necessity would be compounded by a claim of justice.

The case of using dangerous weapons or warheads as leverage for some goods is prone to similar worries. If the cost of someone exercising his right of necessity is that others will have their basic security rights violated or severely threatened, then the latter cannot be requested to express her solidarity towards the former as a proper moral response. Once more, such a requirement would be overdemanding, as the exercise of the right would be dependent on the violation of some other equally important moral interests.[5]

Summing up, I have argued that the content of the right of necessity should not only be limited to material things the use of which is needed for basic subsistence but also include the means to obtain these things. Moreover, I have suggested that, depending on the circumstances, these means need not only be those required to guarantee immediate subsistence but may also include the means required by the agents to become self-sufficient in the long-term.

THE FORM OF THE RIGHT OF NECESSITY

I propose to understand the form of the right of necessity as a *privilege* compounded by a *claim* against others (including the owners of the targeted property) not to interfere with the agent's actions.

To recall, if A has a privilege to φ, A is under no duty not to φ. In the case in point, this means that the needy person is under no duty not to take, use and/or occupy someone else's resources in order to get out of his plight. But privileges alone are weak, because they do not entail any claims against others. As Judith Jarvis Thomson expresses it, 'there is no such thing as infringing a person's right if that right is a privilege. It is clear that ... X's having as regards Y a privilege of doing such and such is entirely compatible with X's having no claim against Y to X's actually doing the such and such, or to Y's assistance in doing the such and such, or even to Y's non-interference with X's doing the such and such'.[6] This is why A's non-relational privilege to φ must be compounded with a relational claim against others to let him φ. This much stronger cluster-right is what Thomson calls a *liberty* proper. If A is at liberty to φ, 'he is under no duty at all not to do it (thus he has a privilege against everyone of doing it) and everyone else is under a duty towards him not to interfere with his doing it in some appropriately chosen set of ways'.[7] That the agent has a *liberty of necessity* thus entails that others are under a duty to refrain from interfering with his actions, even if this implies letting him take, use and/or occupy a slice of their own property.

By interpreting the right of necessity as a liberty of necessity, I set my account between Grotius's and Pufendorf's. With the former, I emphasise the freedom of the agent to pursue the courses of action needed to maintain himself alive, just as he would in a pre-institutional scenario where all things are free for everyone's immediate use and consumption. But this freedom alone is not enough. This is why, with the latter, I emphasise the duty by which all other individuals are bound when what the agent is pursuing is his very self-preservation. This duty is based on two of the normative assumptions presented at the beginning of the book: that no one may be forced to abide by rules the respect of which may threaten one's very self-preservation, and that we owe some minimal duties of solidarity to each other as members of one (global) society.

Correlated Duties

Accepting the exercise of the right of necessity within a cosmopolitan morality implies accepting its correlated duties as well. I classify these duties in two types. One type are duties of non-interference, divided into specific, immediate duties, and general, mediate ones. The other type are final duties not to participate in the creation and/or upholding of conditions where there are people who may permissibly claim necessity, but are at the same time practically incapacitated from so doing, or, positively stated, duties to create conditions where the exercise of the right of necessity by the chronically deprived ceases to exist. Because the aim of this project is above all to set a new normative framework for moral cosmopolitanism within which the right of necessity takes centre stage, here I offer a brief sketch of what each of these duties implies, rather than a thorough account of each.

Regarding duties of non-interference, these concern the specific, immediate duty not to interfere with the agent's actions on the spot, but they also include the general, mediate duty not to make needed resources inaccessible to those who are in a situation such that they may claim them. The specific, immediate duty not to interfere can include, for example, not to stop squatters, encampers or petty-thieves if, given the available evidence, it is reasonable to believe they are in need,[8] and not to report the violation of intellectual property laws if what is at stake is the production of life-saving generic medicines for those who have no other means to access them.[9] When it comes to public servants and officials, may the police choose not to arrest individuals engaged in illegal actions if, given the available evidence, they have good reason to believe they are needy? Or may a jury depart from the rule and acquit legitimate claimants that would have otherwise been criminally prosecuted? I think they should, and that their defence should be based on their not following rules which they deem to be in direct violation of the very interests that those rules are supposed to protect.[10]

In real life, however, many who are in a position to exercise their right of necessity are actually unable to do it—because the resources they need are inaccessible to them. Insofar as one is aware that one is living in a society where this is the case, fulfilling one's general, mediate duty of non-interference requires one not to make resources unavailable for those who may potentially need them. Against the tendency of property owners to secure their belongings behind high bars and ever more sophisticated security systems, this is an appeal, then, to go in the exactly opposite direction. If we are to revive a conception of property rights where these serve first and foremost a social function (i.e., where they are for the benefit of all, rather than some, or even the majority), then this is a necessary step to take. The most obvious way for individuals to fulfil this duty is then not to make one's own property so guarded as to make it impossible for others to access it if needed.

Both specific, immediate duties of non-interference and general, mediate duties of non-interference correlated to the right of necessity should be distinguished from final duties to put an end to chronic deprivation on a global scale. As said in chapter 4, the most important aim when framing the global economic order—and within it, property arrangements—should be to create a society where the exercise of the right of necessity becomes truly exceptional and confined to emergencies, or, put differently, a society where it is not the case that people are placed in a position such that they are morally permitted to claim their right of necessity, but are practically incapacitated to do it. Until that aim is achieved, notwithstanding, the existence of duties of non-interference correlated to the right of necessity has to be acknowledged.[11] (That this might bring about potentially unfair outcomes and further undermine the long-term prospects for becoming the kind of world where subsistence rights are universally fulfiled are weighty objections that I address in chapter 6.)

Before moving on to the next section, something needs to be said regarding the use of force. After all, if the right of necessity is a claimable right, then those who fail to fulfil the correlated duties may be forced to do otherwise, or may they not?

To respond to this it is necessary to distinguish two different kinds of force. If what one has in mind is force as *violence*, then there are strong reasons not to resort to it. As Thomas Pogge rightly points out, talk of violence as a purported solution to global poverty is counterproductive and damaging, and serves as the perfect excuse for those in a position of power to keep things as they are rather than to advance change.[12]

On the other hand, if what one has in mind is force as *resistance*, then I do think that there are reasons to commend it. As said from the outset, claims of necessity for immediate subsistence made by random, disorganised individuals have the potential to turn into the claims of organised social movements with the ability to make more ambitious, long-term demands by resorting to this strategy. Allow me to mention three examples.

The *callamperos* or urban homeless were a group of people in Santiago, Chile, who, between the 1950s and 1970s, became known for occupying empty urban patches overnight. As the historian Mario Garcés recalls, 'These settlements were not occupied *politically*, but out of *necessity*. The person simply arrived and took a place, then others arrived and settled around, and it was thus that they came together'.[13] The callamperos were rarely evicted and, when the authorities tried to pursue this path, they resisted pacifically until the latter gave up. This amounted to a tacit approval of their actions both by the authorities and by the surrounding city dwellers. And, although they were meant to be provisional solutions to the housing crisis, it was often the case that the *callampas* became established as permanent settlements, with their inhabitants progressively coordinating their actions to demand better living conditions.[14]

Another example goes back to the origin of the *Movimento dos Trabalhadores Rurais Sem Terra*, or Movement of Rural Landless Workers (MST), in Brazil. As its founders tell, the movement 'was born from the *concrete, isolated* struggles for land that rural workers were developing in southern Brazil at the end of the 1970s'[15] but soon gained the support of church grassroots organisations, as well as that of the Workers' Political Party. What began as illegal encampments and occupations of vast unused tracts of land that belonged to a few *fazendeiros* (owners of large rural estates) became an organised front that, through pacific resistance and through the employment of legal tools and concepts, sought to revive the forgotten social function of property rights and to give to thousands the possibility of working the land to achieve self-subsistence.[16]

A third case of organised resistance that emerged from the individual claims of the needy were the so-called *water wars* in Bolivia in the early 2000s. First in the city of Cochabamba and afterwards in El Alto, thousands of people continued to collect water from the rain and from their wells when this became illegal, after the water services became privatised. Eventually, in Cochabamba the social movement called *Coordinadora para la Defensa del Agua y de la Vida* succeeded in forcing the multinational water companies to retreat, and demanded the establishment of democratic, public water facilities with active communal involvement instead.[17]

Opting for resistance instead of violence, moreover, has an important expressive value for the legitimation of the needy's actions amidst those who might otherwise fear them and drift even further apart from them. With this in mind, it is force as resistance rather than force as violence which should be commended.[18]

THREE CONDITIONS

In this section I propose that three conditions are necessary and jointly sufficient for the right of necessity to be invoked. These are that the need in question is indeed basic, the person in need does not violate other equally important moral interests to exercise her right, and this moral prerogative is appealed to as a last resort.[19]

The fulfilment of these conditions is important if what one wishes to defend is the right of necessity understood as generating duties on others, and not merely as a privilege to act with no guarantees that the agent will not be interfered with in so doing.

I have already referred to what I understand by subsistence needs, how they concern the physical and physiological aspects of well-being, and why they should be the object of a basic right. One might worry here, however, that the account given is too modest. By limiting what the needy may claim via the right of necessity only to those provisions required for survival, I seem to be letting off the hook property systems that might be extremely unfair, so long as they ensure that their members do not starve to death. With these standards, some might complain, even a slave society could pass the test. But, quoting the famous words of American abolitionist Solomon Northup, 'I don't want to *survive*; I want to live!'

I do not deny that more than the basics for survival may be claimed as a matter of right, but the arguments given to support those claims are different in kind than those offered to uphold the right to subsistence via the right of necessity. I am not saying that all rights-claims end once subsistence has been secured; I am merely saying that subsistence is such a basic human interest that individuals should be allowed to do (almost) whatever they need in order to secure it, even if this means breaking the standard rules. My aim thus is to highlight the moral wrong of denying the exercise of the right of necessity even to those who lack those things necessary to subsist; to show why it is morally problematic to require people to act on principles fit for Overland (a society where all individuals have their basic rights respected, protected and fulfiled under normal circumstances) while still living in Underland (a society where individuals are expected to abide by the rules even if these go against the fulfilment of their basic rights).

That the needy person may not, through the exercise of her right, violate other equally important moral interests is a second, blocking condition that rules out two possibilities: on the one hand, it prevents the needy person from exercising her right against someone equally needy or who will end up equally needy in the same relevant respect; on the other hand, it prevents the needy agent from exercising her right in such a way that compromises other equally important moral interests—paradigmatically, other people's or her own basic liberties or security rights.

Unless this condition is upheld, the right of necessity is prone to becoming something like the Hobbesian *right of nature*: the power that every person has for his own preservation in the original state of nature, which for Hobbes is a state of war. This right is 'a right to everything, even to another's body. And therefore, as long as this natural right of every man to everything endureth, there can be no security to any man (how strong or wise soever he be)'.[20] This is also, to recall, one of the objections posed by Pufendorf against his interpretation of the Grotian right of necessity as a mere privilege, where might makes right and there seem to be no limits either to what the needy person may do or to how the owner of the targeted resources may respond. Contrariwise, the proposed understanding of the right of necessity as a liberty requires that the latter are able to respond without thereby compromising their own equally important moral interests. In other words, if we take the right of necessity to create a correlated duty on others (including the owner of the targeted resources), it would be contradictory—or, as will be explained in more detail in chapter 6, *theoretically overdemanding*—to require those upon whom the duty falls to do something by virtue of which they will end up in a similar or worse situation than the one they are trying to remedy.[21]

Depending on how one looks at it, this second condition might seem too demanding or too lax for the claimant. On the one hand, if a person is in real need and she has no other way to get out of her plight but to take the resources of those who are equally (or almost as) needy, would it not be too taxing to demand that she abstain from encroaching upon the property of the other person? To this, my reply is the same I give in the course of interpreting Pufendorf's condition that 'this license can by no means take place if the owner of the thing which we want, lies under as great a necessity as we ourselves'.[22] For it to create a correlated duty on others (specifically, on the owners of the target of appropriation) without it becoming overdemanding, the right of necessity may be exercised only against those who are materially better-off, and without violating the latter's basic liberties—assuming, as has been repeated time and again, that they have not been directly implicated in the agent's plight. I have given arguments as to why any reasonable system of property rights must include the right of necessity as an internal limitation; those same arguments can be used to show why no reasonable system of property rights can demand people to comply with a duty that comes at the cost of sacrificing their own, equally important moral interests.[23]

On the other hand, by setting the threshold of those from whom one may claim one's right so low, there is a risk that the systematic exercise of this right by the needy might contribute to grossly unfair outcomes, where those just a bit above the threshold fall all the way down to it, only to raise those below the threshold to the minimum acceptable. In other words, the extremely poor would seem to be granted a right to take from the very poor, while the latter acquire a duty to let their scant belongings be taken from them. Furthermore, in the actual world, this is in all likelihood what would happen, given that those with less resources are also less able to protect them—leaving those with more and better guarded resources almost entirely off their reach.[24]

Commonsensical at first sight, what is troubling about this objection is that it turns the problem on its head. To affirm that, by allowing the exercise of the right of necessity the needy will end up harming others in a similar position, and to conclude therefore that this right should not be upheld, is to put the burden on the wrong shoulders. As repeatedly stressed, the point of discussing at length the proper place of the right of necessity in the global poverty debate is precisely as a response to the continued failure to guarantee, first and foremost, access to certain minimal material provisions, or to the means of obtaining them, for all individuals. So long as this does not happen, it is not reasonable to require the needy to wait passively until others fulfil their duties towards them, as I expound in more detail in chapter 6. Moreover, it could be added that this objection ignores a whole body of literature in human geography that points exactly in the opposite direction—namely, to how those chronically deprived tend to create partnerships to solve their predicament, rather than act to the detriment of those in a similar situation.[25]

A third necessary condition for the right of necessity to be exercised is that it has to be appealed to as a last resort, after other paths of action that could have been pursued with a reasonable chance of success have failed (this includes taking into consideration the least cost-imposing methods available to exercise one's right). These can include searching for a job, directly asking for assistance, appealing to the relevant authorities, and engaging in political action, insofar as these are realistic options for the person in need.

The last resort condition seems fairly uncontroversial: it sounds sensible to limit the right of necessity by making sure that the agents will only have recourse to it after trying other less disruptive options. Still, a possible objection is that, given the epistemic limitations of the agents, it might not be transparent to them when this condition has been fulfilled: maybe they don't know that there are other options open to them before resorting to claiming necessity; maybe they know that there are other options, but these do not seem as certain and definite as appealing to necessity; maybe they are mistaken about the urgency of their need and invoke their right instead of looking for other alternatives.

To this I respond that epistemic limitations are not a problem for judgments of this kind only, but for moral judgments in general. Moreover, if we take the epistemic limitation of agents into consideration, then this condition could be rephrased thus: that the right of necessity should be appealed to only as a last resort, where what counts as last resort is what a reasonable person would count as such, given the evidence that the needy agent would have if he had conscientiously searched for it, insofar as this was possible for him. While, in some cases, it will not be obvious that the agents have tried hard enough to look for alternative solutions, there will be others where the direness of the situation and the description of the context will point pretty clearly in this direction.[26]

This appeal to reasonableness serves to discard as viable options activities or occupations that go against the agent's deeply held moral beliefs, or affect the basic moral interests of other people or of the agent herself.

On the one hand, one might think of someone conscientiously objecting to being a surrogate mother, to slaughtering animals in a factory farm, or to engaging in street prostitution, if these seem to be the only opportunities open to them in the job market. Here, paraphrasing Bernard Williams, one could say that forcing the needy to take up these jobs would be to make *one demand too many* upon them. If one truly endorses a cosmopolitan morality such that every individual human being is considered as an ultimate unit of moral concern, then respecting their basic liberty to refuse to engage in activities that they find deeply morally damaging seems like a minimal standard to be followed. On the other hand, not to engage in activities that damage other people's or one's own basic moral interests rules out businesses like selling highly addictive drugs to well-off customers or trading one's corneas and kidneys in the black market.

Relatedly, there is the question of how precarious a type of economic occupation must be for it to be ruled out as an alternative path. While self-enslavement seems obviously unacceptable, one might ask whether sweatshop work, for example, should be considered before resorting to the right of necessity. Here again one should focus on the basic moral interests of the individual and see whether they are respected or not. The deficient working conditions (with elemental health standards and security measures ignored), the long working hours, the meagre wages (sometimes below subsistence levels), and the weak or non-existent enforcement of labour laws (which allows for abusive treatment by bosses, sexual harassment and use of children and youngsters) defy the claim that sweatshops are a reasonable option for those who have no other. The most tragic example to prove this point was the structural collapse of the Rana Plaza, an eight-story building in Dhaka, Bangladesh, which left more than 1,100 workers dead and many more injured in April 2013.[27]

How many other occupations fit a similar pattern — with below subsistence-level wages, poor working conditions, and/or exploitative relationships between bosses and workers, or between clients and workers? While this is not the place to develop such an inquiry, depending on the answer given the argument here offered would have massive practical implications, which so far remain unexplored.

CONCLUDING REMARKS

In this chapter I defined the right of necessity as a right to take, use and/or occupy those material resources required for subsistence, or the means to obtain the former. I then explained why the privilege of necessity has to be supplemented by a claim of non-interference against others, making this right a liberty proper. Because the right of necessity thus understood correlates to immediate duties on the part of others, I spelled out three necessary and jointly sufficient conditions for its exercise: that the need must be basic, that the agent must not violate other equally important moral interests by exercising her right, and that it must be a last resort.

That accepting the exercise of this right within a cosmopolitan morality might be a *remedy worse than the disease* is a central objection that I began to address in this chapter and continue to elaborate in the next one. There I systematise the main worries of accepting the right of necessity within a cosmopolitan morality.

NOTES

1. Whereas all the other material resources needed to subsist are things that may be appropriated by others and from whose access we can therefore be excluded, breathable air is still an exception (for how access to it is going to become one of the most serious ethical issues in space colonisation, however, see Charles Cockell, *Extraterrestrial Liberty: An Enquiry into the Nature and Causes of Tyrannical Government beyond the Earth* [Edinburgh: Shoving Leopard, 2013], 15). Having said this, if the air pollution in a place becomes so bad as to endanger the lives of its inhabitants (by seriously affecting their health or by seriously damaging their means of subsistence—for example, by killing their crops), I suggest that these people have a claim of necessity to move and resettle. In cases where the agents themselves can be shown to be responsible for the pollution, I suggest that they would still have a right to resettle, but would also have duties of compensation towards their hosts.

2. I thank Gillian Brock for suggesting these examples. A related objection regards the question of how indirect the relationship could be between what is claimed and what is ultimately required as a matter of necessity. That is, one might ask whether it is also part of the content of this right whatever is a means to the means of subsistence, and so on and so forth, *ad infinitum*. To this I reply that, rather than trying to figure out hard and fast rules regarding how many steps away from the objective something may be claimed as a legitimate means, one should check instead whether those steps are conducive to the satisfaction of the agent's basic needs and are, insofar as possible, the least cost-imposing ones. Going back to the hiker-in-the-storm example with a slight variation: imagine that the cabin which the hiker is trying to enter is so hermetically closed that she needs to use—and maybe also wreck—a pair of skis from a third party to break a window to then get in. Nobody would object, in this case, that she did not have a claim of necessity to use the skis because the skis were not directly needed for her to get out of her plight, but were only a means to the means to the end. And the same would apply, I think, if she had needed still something else to get the skis in the first place. As long as the chain of means led her to a safe haven to pass the storm in the least cost-imposing way available, it would be hard to argue against her right to take, use and/or occupy any of them—provided, also, that she did not violate any other equally important moral interests in the way, which is one of the conditions for the right to be exercised, as I explain below.

3. As A. John Simmons puts it, ownership should be limited to those things that we use, and that are centrally related to our purposive activities, and no more. Although his analysis concerns Locke's theory specifically, it is a useful criterion to measure the reasonable limits of property in general: A. John Simmons, *The Lockean Theory of Rights* (Princeton, NJ: Princeton University Press, 1992), 276–77.

4. See 'Podemos propone expropiar todas las viviendas vacías y legalizar la "okupación"', *Libremercado*, June 4, 2014, accessed November 30, 2015, http://www.

libremercado.com/2014-06-04/podemos-propone-expropiar-todas-las-viviendas-vacias-y-legalizar-la-okupacion-1276520311/; and 'La juez absuelve a los primeros ocupas de la Corrala Utopía', *El País*, September 25, 2015, accessed November 30, 2015, http://politica.elpais.com/politica/2015/09/25/actualidad/1443180509_667442.html.

5. Adam Smith once said that, although a linen shirt is 'strictly speaking, not a necessary of life ... in the present times, through the greater part of Europe, a creditable day-labourer would be ashamed to appear in public without a linen shirt, the want of which would be supposed to denote that disgraceful degree of poverty which, it is presumed, nobody can well fall into without extreme bad conduct': Adam Smith, *An Inquiry into the Nature and Causes of the Wealth of Nations*, ed. Edwin Cannan, vol. 2 (London: Methuen & Co, 1904), V.II.2.4, 354. What Smith omitted from his analysis was the plausible conclusion that maybe, then, the workers' right to subsistence ought to include a right to a linen shirt, insofar as without it they would be condemned to live as outcasts. In the same spirit, one could ask today whether in highly industrialised economies, for example, things like a mobile phone or PC, a basic wardrobe, or elementary education may be claimed as means to have one's basic subsistence needs met. Although I do not focus on these kinds of cases, I grant that, so long as it could be shown that one's individual subsistence depends on one being able to be integrated into the social system, and so long as it could be shown that being able to integrate oneself into the social system depends on one's access to certain specific material things, one may have a right of necessity to these indirect means of subsistence, too.

6. Thomson, *Realm of Rights*, 47.

7. Thomson, *Realm of Rights*, 54.

8. See, for example, Diane Taylor, 'Manchester United Stars Neville and Giggs Tell Hotel Squatters: Stay for Winter', *Guardian*, October 19, 2015, accessed January 22, 2016, http://www.theguardian.com/society/2015/oct/18/former-manchester-united-star-occupiers-of-hotel-winter-ryan-giggs-gary-neville.

9. India's government decision to allow domestic companies to produce generic versions of patented pharmaceuticals developed in other countries goes in this direction. See, however, how it might end due to pressure from the latter: Holger Krahmer, 'India's Lawless War on Intellectual Property', *Wall Street Journal*, March 23, 2014, http://www.wsj.com/articles/SB10001424052702304679404579456672440016300/; and 'India: Health Activists Fear Decreased Access to Medicines for the Poor—as Government Reviews Intellectual Property Laws', Business and Human Rights Resource Centre, October 8, 2014, http://business-humanrights.org/en/india-health-activists-fear-decreased-access-to-medicines-for-the-poor-as-govt-reviews-intellectual-property-laws, both accessed January 22, 2016.

10. For an actual case, see Tobias Salinger, 'Police Officer Who Caught Homeless Mom Stealing for Children at Walmart Buys Diapers, Wipes, Shoes for Her', *New York Daily News*, July 11, 2015, accessed November 30, 2015, http://www.nydailynews.com/news/crime/caught-homeless-mom-stealing-buys-diapers-article-1.2289506.

11. In fact, even if this goal is achieved, a place must be left for the performance of these duties in cases of one-off emergencies.

12. See Pogge, 'Poverty and Violence', 109–10.

13. Garcés, *Tomando su sitio*, 38; my translation and emphases added.

14. There are, around the world, less successful stories of similar undertakings. See, for example, the case of the illegal settlements euphemistically called *novostroiki* (*new constructions*) in Bishkek, Kyrgyzstan, where the dwellers lack residence permits and as a result are practically disenfranchised socially and politically: Balihar Sanghera and Elmira Satybaldieva, 'Ethics of Property, Illegal Settlements and the Right to Subsistence', *International Journal of Sociology and Social Policy* 32, 1/2 (2012): 102ff. See also the case of the largest illegal urban settlement in Africa, Kibera, in Nairobi, Kenya. With over 900,000 inhabitants, it has only recently begun to be acknowledged by the authorities but still lacks the most basic services: Emmanuel Mutisya and Masaru Yarime, 'Understanding the Grassroots Dynamics of Slums in Nairobi: The Dilemma of Kibera Informal Settlements', *International Transaction Journal of Engineering, Man-*

agement, & Applied Sciences & Technologies 2, 2 (2011). Rather than as counterexamples, these should be seen as current instances where the right of necessity of the people ought to be upheld and regarded as a legitimate first step towards the fulfilment of their basic housing needs.

15. Friends of the MST, 'History of the MST', http://www.mstbrazil.org/content/history-mst, accessed October 16, 2015; emphasis added.

16. George Meszaros, 'Taking the Land into Their Hands: The Landless Workers' Movement and the Brazilian State', *Journal of Law and Society* 27, 4 (2000): 518. See also Robin Dunford, who proposes that the actions of the MST and La Via Campesina (International Peasant's Movement) are instances where the needy themselves are enacting their rights and thereby defying their depiction as quiet and powerless recipients of aid: Robin Dunford, 'Human Rights and Collective Emancipation: The Politics of Food Sovereignty', *Review of International Studies* 41, 2 (2014).

17. Madeline Baer, 'From Water Wars to Water Rights: Implementing the Human Right to Water in Bolivia', *Journal of Human Rights* 14, 3 (2015).

18. South American liberation theology is a rich source when it comes to the conceptualisation of resistance as a driving force behind poor-led movements. See, for example, 'Our starting point is the capacity to resist and the life force of the poorest and the outcast. We must learn from the accumulated experience of the oppressed ... We must learn from the experiences of life and organisation by those who have been left out of the neoliberal system. We must learn from the people's economy of solidarity in what are called the "informal sectors." We must learn from women, especially the poorest, who have always borne the whole burden of survival and who in this century have emerged as social actors within the current system. We must learn from their wisdom, from the lowly, from those who endure social pain, those who observe and suffer present society from the outside and from below': Pablo Richard, 'A Theology of Life: Rebuilding Hope from the Perspective of the South', in *Spirituality of the Third World: A Cry for Life*, ed. K. C. Abraham and Bernadette Mbuy-Beya (Eugene, OR: Wipf and Stock, 2005), 97.

19. This account is inspired by, but not fully faithful to, Grotius's list of *admonitions* and Pufendorf's list of *conditions* regarding who should be granted this right, and how this right should be exercised. Cf. Grotius, *The Law of War and Peace (DJB)* II.II.6, 194–95; and Pufendorf, *The Law of Nature and Nations (DJN)* II.VI, 209. I leave out, however, the conditions of moral innocence of the agent and restitution. Regarding moral innocence, I take it that it is just as intractable to precisely determine the degree of responsibility of the agents for their own plight as it is to determine their degree of responsibility in the plight of others. As for restitution, I think it makes sense to include it as an ex post duty in one-off cases of necessity (like those that would arise in Overland) but not in cases where necessity is claimed by the chronically deprived. If anyone, here it should be other potential duty-bearers and not the needy agents who ought to compensate those mediately or immediately bearing their duties of non-interference. I say more on these compensatory duties in chapter 6.

20. Thomas Hobbes, *Leviathan*, ed. Noel Malcolm, vol. 2 (Oxford: Clarendon Press, 2012), 198.

21. The term *theoretical overdemandingness* is from Jan-Christoph Heilinger, 'The Moral Demandingness of Socioeconomic Human Rights', in *The Philosophy of Human Rights: Contemporary Controversies*, ed. Jan-Christoph Heilinger and Gerhard Ernst (Berlin: De Gruyter, 2012), 196ff. Here again it has to be reminded that claims of necessity must be kept separate from claims of justice. If the potential duty-bearer were directly responsible for the plight of the agent, then the latter may be permitted to demand much more from the former, and the legitimate use of force would not be straightforwardly ruled out. What if the potential duty-bearers are not directly responsible for the claimant's plight but refuse to comply with their duty not to interfere? I think that this kind of case is analogous to cases where initially innocent bystanders who fail to assist someone at t_1 may be (proportionately) enforced to do so at t_2. In other words, because of their initial failure to comply they may be subjected to the

proportionate use of force at a later time. See Christian Barry and Gerhard Øverland, 'The Implications of Failing to Assist', *Social Theory and Practice* 40, 4 (2014).

22. Pufendorf, *DJN* II.VI.6, 209.

23. Some might propose here that the morally advisable procedure would be for the owner of the sought resources to accept tossing a coin and let luck decide. It seems to me more accurate to say that, in scenarios of this kind, what agents have is a mere privilege, rather than a full-blown liberty of necessity.

24. For how this is already happening, see '[In Latin American cities,] two peripheries have emerged: an inclusive and an exclusive one. In the city's margins one can find secluded, private condos, but also shantytowns, *favelas*, marginal settlements, *lost cities* ... in sum, ghettos of poverty and marginalization, where need, hunger, casual work or no work at all have come to stay. Where do the people who inhabit these *lost cities* go to? And those who see on a daily basis the face of need, of overcrowding, of hunger, of misery: what are they waiting for? What do those who are included in the system do for those who are not? Everything seems to indicate that they drift further away. They lock themselves up in their closed, private spaces, not to face poverty, not to clash against the enemy, the potential aggressor, the face that portrays insecurity': Paola Bonavitta and Marcos Servín Valencia, 'Las ciudades de los excluidos en una Latinoamérica posmoderna', *Kairos: Revista de Temas Sociales* 29 (2012), 2–3; my translation.

25. See, for example, David Harvey, 'The Culture of Poverty: An Ideological Analysis', *Sociological Perspectives* 39, 4 (1996): 490.

26. Actually, this epistemic requirement can be built into the other two conditions as well, considering that the agent might not be entirely certain as to what constitutes basic need, or he might be wrong in judging if, by exercising his right, he will be violating some equally important moral interests of others. I thank Stephanie Collins for suggesting this point.

27. 'Rana Plaza Arrangement', accessed November 30, 2015, http://www.ranaplaza-arrangement.org/. While the most tragic, this was neither the only nor the last episode in a systematic economic practice that keeps producing basic rights violations. See, for example, Institute for Global Labour and Human Rights and Federation of Independent Associations and Unions of El Salvador, 'Dressing Babies in Sweatshop Clothing: Dallas Cowboys, Ohio State and a Creepy Business', Joint Report, October 2011, http://www.globallabourrights.org/reports/document/1110-IGLHR-DressingBabiesInSweatshopClothing-StyleAvenue-1.pdf; and Patrick Winn, 'Here's How the Cambodians Who Stitch Your Clothes Are Routinely Abused', *Global Post*, March 19, 2015, http://www.globalpost.com/dispatch/news/regions/asia-pacific/cambodia/150319/the-cambodians-who-stitch-your-clothes-routinely-abused-exploited, both accessed January 22, 2016.

SIX
The Overdemandingness Objection

In a society where the satisfaction of the basic needs of everyone is not guaranteed, but where property rules are enforced against everyone equally, my contention in the last chapter was that those in a deprived situation have a liberty against others to those resources required to satisfy their basic needs. This liberty is a cluster-right composed of two different incidents of rights: a privilege, which leaves the needy person under no duty not to take, use and/or occupy someone else's property, if this is required to get out of her plight; and a claim against others (including the owner of the targeted resources) not to make the resources needed inaccessible for her, and to let her freely proceed. In practice, this means that if a group of homeless people occupy an empty building, the owner should let them stay; that if someone who it is reasonable to believe is needy takes one's wallet, one should not report him to the police; that if a person does not have enough money to pay for the electricity bill, and she lives in a place where electricity is needed for heating and cooking, she may tap into the electricity supply, and she ought not to be reported. Furthermore, I suggested that the duties immediately and mediately correlated to the right of necessity ought to be distinguished from the final duty not to create and/or uphold conditions under which people may permissibly claim necessity while being at the same time practically unable to do it, or—positively stated—the duty to create conditions under which they are no longer put in that situation.

These possibilities immediately conjure upon non-needy readers 'fantasies of pauperization',[1] and the fear of becoming suckers in a scenario where everyone seems to be waiting for everyone else to act before they do anything themselves. It might also be objected that, while non-interference is a relatively cheap and easy duty to comply with when it correlates to liberty rights, it is not so when it correlates to the right of necessity as I propose to understand it. Non-interference here, after all, implies letting the chronically deprived come and encroach upon your own belongings, which you have earned through hard work and lots of effort, things to which you should be fully entitled. Or should you?

In what follows, I address in more detail different angles of the objection that the right of necessity and its correlated duty might constitute an overdemanding moral principle, especially for the duty-bearers, but maybe also for the claimants themselves. It is important to note that these specific criticisms are not to be found in the existing body of global justice and global assistance literature but have rather emerged from audiences and readers to whom different parts of this book have been presented. As already said, the idea that the right of necessity for the chronically deprived has a place in the contemporary debate on global poverty and moral cosmopolitanism is yet undeveloped, and so is the conceptualisation of the problems attached to such an idea.[2]

To proceed, I loosely base my account on Jan-Christoph Heilinger's typology of *overdemanding* moral principles, which evaluates the latter starting from the idea that 'it is a necessary condition of being morally obliged to do something that we are *able* to do it or can be *reasonably expected* to do it'.[3] After explaining what each kind of overdemandingness comprises (namely, *epistemic*, *psychological* and *theoretical*), I examine how the right of necessity and its correlated duty fare. I conclude that, while these objections are serious ones, the right of necessity should nonetheless be upheld as an escape valve for those confronting continued deprivation.

EPISTEMIC OVERDEMANDINGNESS

A moral principle is epistemically overdemanding if the agent cannot know what the correct action is under a complex set of circumstances. Confronted with a given situation, then, she does not have enough knowledge of the background and/or the particulars to make a well-informed decision.[4]

How does this charge apply to the right of necessity and its correlated duty? Are they impossible to determine in the sense just defined?

When it comes to the right-holder, one might ask whether it is possible for her to know whether the owner of the targeted resources is in such a position that letting these resources be taken will not leave the latter in an equally (or almost as equally) deprived situation. Alternatively, one might worry that the true epistemic challenge is not so much for prospective claimants but for prospective duty-bearers. How can I, the property owner, know after all that the person invoking a right of necessity to my resources is truly needy and not just badly off or, worse, plainly an impostor? Why should I let someone who *appears* to be needy run away with my handbag and do nothing about it? And why should I believe the story of someone who takes money from me and demands not to be stopped on the grounds that she is chronically deprived?

From the standpoint of the needy agent, most of the time it should not be hard to determine whether the owner of the targeted resources is in an equally diminished situation. Notwithstanding, it might often be the case that the needy end up targeting the resources of those who are just a bit better-off than them (rather than much better-off), or that they choose the resources of someone whose property has been repeatedly targeted in the past (because, for example, it is easier to access), rather than the property of someone who has never been targeted before. There is an epistemic challenge, then, in choosing potential duty-bearers in a way that is as fair as possible.

As already explained, however, the primary aim of the right of necessity is to achieve the individual's self-preservation rather than long-term social justice—even if, as shown in chapter 5, acting on the right of necessity might in fact indirectly contribute to the latter. In this sense, even if the right-holder were unable to obtain the sort of information that he would need in order to make the fairest choice, he should still be permitted to act. That this is a disturbing consequence of allowing the exercise of this right should not be seen as a reason to deter potential claimants, but rather as a reason to prevent people from falling into such a deprived state in the first place. The importance of structural adjustments of the sort needed to make the exercise of the right of necessity a true exception comes back into the picture: to avoid arbitrariness in terms of who is targeted, and to avoid the permanent uncertainty for potential duty-bearers, achieving universal compliance with this final duty should be the top desideratum of a cosmopolitan morality (however, an idea for how to diminish the potential unfairness of the principle is proposed in the next section).

Regarding the epistemic challenge for prospective duty-bearers, this worry is based, first of all, on a questionable assumption—namely, that pretending to be needy to thus make a living out of repeatedly taking other people's property is a tempting way of life that many would happily adopt if the right of necessity gained universal acceptance. This ignores the psychological aversion that people normally have against theft, as well as their fear of being not only prosecuted by the law but also socially marginalised; above all, it ignores that most people simply want *to have a life*. Moreover, this worry is triggered by the idea that there is no upper limit as to what the needy may take from others. But there is: as stressed in chapter 5, the exercise of this right is reserved for those in a situation of continued deprivation to go and look for the means of exiting that state, and no more. This sets quite tight bounds to what the needy may claim.[5]

There are two more things to say concerning the epistemic challenge for potential duty-bearers. First of all, and especially in the case of those who are sufficiently well-off (so that their lives will not suffer any major disruptions if they discharge their duty), I suggest that it is better to err on the side of caution. In other words, when not entirely sure about the situation of the person claiming her right, the property owner should insofar as possible abstain from interfering. Given what might be at stake, this should be the morally preferred course of action. Second, and more important, I think that a way to address this challenge is to establish some sort of protocol between claimants and potential duty-bearers. By this I mean that, whenever possible, both parties should strive to be as candid, attentive and informative as possible about their respective situations, as well as respectful of each other's basic interests. This will sound shockingly naïve, especially to those who tend to suspect, rather than rely on, other human beings, and who fear that letting the needy get their way will put them in a disadvantaged position vis-à-vis others who refuse to do likewise. In my view, such a sceptical response has to do with the fact that abstract, impersonal talk of human rights has blinded agents to the possibility of actually encountering those whose rights remain unfulfiled and towards whom they may have immediate duties. The direct confrontation—or, better, contact—between agents, and what it generates morally, is an aspect of the discussion that has been very much absent in the literature on global justice and global assistance. When these encounters happen, the default procedure so far has been to require the needy to put themselves in the shoes of property owners and therefore to abstain from encroaching upon the latter's belongings. In a scenario where the right of necessity came to be acknowledged, by contrast, property owners and other parties would put themselves in the shoes of the chronically deprived and take that experience into account when making the decision of whether to comply with their duty. Eventually, this could lead them to change their attitude to these kinds of takings and to accept them, so to speak, as a self-imposed tax that fulfils an important function in the absence of globally enforced mechanisms designed for this end.

PSYCHOLOGICAL OVERDEMANDINGNESS

A moral principle can be psychologically overdemanding in three ways. It can be too costly as such if it requires huge sacrifices from agents, to the point where they have to postpone their own personal projects and relationships, and even their well-being, to satisfy it. It can also be too costly for specific agents under conditions of generalised non-compliance (by being insensitive to what other individuals do or fail to do in order to diminish the suffering of the poor, Peter Singer's *principle of assistance* has been criticised precisely on this front). Finally, a moral principle can be said to be too costly if the moral character of the agent has been shaped by imperfect institutions, making it hard for her to comply with what moral ideals demand.[6]

I contend that the principle of necessity might be accused of being overdemanding in the second sense, but not in the first or third. It is not overdemanding as such, because in a world in which the universal right to subsistence under normal circumstances is respected, protected and fulfiled, the exercise of the right of necessity by the chronically deprived simply disappears.[7] Regarding the third sense, in a society where property rights are defended almost with no exceptions, and where the majority of people feel fully entitled to every last bit of their belongings, it might seem difficult to require them to let their property be taken away by others for the sake of morality. In general, however, arguments that appeal to the purportedly fixed moral qualities of agents are suspicious, and all the more when they are used as an excuse not to perform actions that might inconvenience them to a greater or lesser extent. It is indeed comfortable to invoke one's upbringing as a reason for not performing one's moral duties, but this does not make the reason any more justifiable. Instead, what morality requires many times is to get agents out of their comfort zone and into the shoes of those who haven't had the luck to step into one. In the case in point, as already signalled, something that has been systematically lacking is a candid attempt by those who are in a privileged socioeconomic position to sympathise with those who are not. By *sympathy* here, I do not mean simply *feeling with the other* but a more complex process engaging both our emotional and our cognitive capacities, an honest attempt to see things from the point of view of the other.[8]

But the principle of necessity advocated might be deemed to be psychologically overdemanding in the second respect. This concerns the effects for prospective duty-bearers who feel *particularly* obligated to perform an action that many other agents, who could have been potentially obligated, fail to perform.[9] More generally, this is the problem of whether and to what extent one should comply with moral principles in non-ideal settings. I call this the *Why Me?* objection.

Why Me?

The discussion of what our moral duties are under generalised non-compliance is a hot topic in moral and political philosophy.[10] The main complaint is that it seems unreasonable to expect agents to do more (and maybe much more) than what their fair share would be under conditions of generalised compliance. When it comes to fulfilling the right of necessity of others, it is easy to see how this duty might turn out to be psychologically overdemanding. Imagine that the prospective duty-bearer owns a farm in the vicinity of a very large slum. As a result, his property gets targeted again and again by the needy, so much so that he ends up in almost as bad a position as the slum dwellers. Although each individual act of appropriation may be permissible considered in isolation, then, the possibility of iterative takings can make the principle of necessity psychologically overdemanding for those whose property is targeted.

This is, in fact, a problematic outcome that the principle of necessity leaves open in principle. Insofar as it allows for the exercise of disorganised, uncoordinated claims, abiding by it might well disadvantage duty-bearers to the point where they end up in a situation almost as dire as the one they are helping to remedy. This is possible because—as just seen—the principle neither precludes the possibility of iterative takings nor ranks among those whose resources may be targeted. By failing to do this, the objection would go, it grants excessive discretion to the claimants to select the people whose property they will take to meet their subsistence needs, creating a host of potentially unfair outcomes.

Indeed, the exercise of the right of necessity is limited only by the three conditions expounded in chapter 5—namely, that the resources claimed must be those required to satisfy subsistence needs; that the basic moral interests of others (or of the agent herself) must not be violated in the way; and that it is only to be resorted to after other reasonable paths of action have been unsuccessfully pursued. These three conditions must be satisfied in order for the right to be a proper claim, the fulfilment of which creates a duty on others. Having as its limited goal the satisfaction of the individual's right to subsistence, over and above these requirements, there is no explicit prescription regarding whom the needy may take from.

In practice, nonetheless, one could build into the principle a double-tiered *recommendation* concerning the desirable profile of the owner of the targeted resources; a recommendation that should be followed inasmuch as possible by the claimants (that is, without it constituting a proper *condition*). It could run as follows: First, 'the agent has good reason to believe that the owner of the targeted resources has not come repeatedly under similar pressure such as to constitute a morally important burden for him/her'.[11] And second, 'the agent has good reason to believe that the socioeconomic position of the intended target of appropriations relative to others is as high and/or as comfortable as possible'; in Pufendorf's words, 'we suppose the owner to abound'.[12] While the former tier prevents the possibility of iterative takings, the latter helps to allocate the immediate duty on those who will be least affected by the loss of resources.[13]

But here the epistemic challenge resurfaces: even if one concedes that it is possible in most cases for agents to know whether the owners of the targeted resources are (almost) as badly off as them, it might not be so easy to know who—among the possible targets—would constitute the fairest choice, and if the latter would be willing to let their resources be taken. I suggest that one way to deflect this worry is to stress the distinction between immediate and mediate duties, on the one hand, and compensatory duties, on the other. The exercise of the right of necessity creates an immediate correlated duty on the owners of the targeted resources and maybe also on third parties not to intervene with the agent's actions, as well as a mediate duty not to create conditions under which potential claimants are deprived from accessing the resources needed. At the same time, it is plausible to say that those who have borne these duties may demand that others who could have also been potentially targeted, but were not for various reasons (for example, because their property was inaccessible to the needy) share the burden with them ex post.[14] These two kinds of duty should not be mistaken for the final duty to prevent chronic deprivation from occurring first and foremost.

At this point, two further objections might be raised. First, some might complain that what I am here suggesting is utterly impracticable and out of touch with reality. If people generally fail to comply with their final duty to fulfil everyone's right to subsistence, why would one expect them to voluntarily succor those who are individually bearing a brunt that should have been collectively distributed from the outset? Why should we suppose that the general landscape of non-compliance when it comes to fulfilling the final duty to prevent deprivation from happening will turn into compliance when it comes to fulfilling a new category of compensatory duties towards others who have played their part?

There are two ways to answer this question. One is to admit that there is in fact no reason to think that things will change, and that therefore the landscape does not look too promising for potential immediate duty-bearers. But, even if this is the case, there is a possibility that, for their own benefit, the latter could push together with the needy for an institutional change. If both sides realise that they are in the same boat and start rowing together in the same direction, the likelihood for structural changes to happen would be greater than if the needy are left alone with their demands. A different answer, and the one I favour, is that there is no reason to assume that our moral characters are inalterable. If the idea that the exercise of the right of necessity is permissible for those chronically deprived becomes increasingly accepted and widespread, the social function of property will also become more salient, presumably leading us to rethink our current arrangements and to relax our current attitudes towards owning things.

A second objection might be posed by those sympathetic to O'Neill's position, saying that the problem I purported to solve in chapter 4 has not been solved at all. I claimed there that, by accepting the exercise of the right of necessity within cosmopolitan morality, the needy themselves specified the relevant duty-bearers—thereby surmounting O'Neill's critique of the human right to subsistence having no correlative, allocated duties. By distinguishing between immediate, mediate, compensatory and final duties, it might be argued that I have only kicked the key question one step further: although the claimants of the right of necessity single out immediate duty-bearers, this does not solve the main problem, which is how to allocate duties correlated to the basic right to subsistence in a fair, equitable way in the middle and long-term. What is more, bringing into the picture new categories of duties makes matters even more complicated: apart from having to allocate the final duty correlated to the basic right to subsistence (which is a hard enough task), now it will also have to be figured out who should compensate whom for the performance of immediate and mediate duties!

To this I reply that, while I concur that our final duties to fulfil the basic right to subsistence are currently unallocated, I disagree with the idea that, insofar as this is the case, the basic right to subsistence remains pure rhetoric. By introducing the exercise of the right of necessity as an escape valve through which those in need may get the resources they require, I am not solving the *big question* of how to reform and rebuild the global institutional system in a way that the satisfaction of basic needs is guaranteed for all and for good. But that was not among the purposes of this book. Rather, among the purposes was to show that, even if accepting such a right within cosmopolitan morality brings with it complications, these should be accepted, and should serve as a forceful reason for making the answer to the *big question* a pressing moral task. This project is thus not the end, but rather the beginning of a different kind of thinking about our cosmopolitan rights and duties than what has been carried out so far, a kind of thinking where acceptance of the right of necessity as a right of those chronically deprived serves as a moral compass with which to re-examine and re-evaluate the *big question*.

THEORETICAL OVERDEMANDINGNESS

A moral principle is theoretically overdemanding if it is self-defeating — that is, if what it requires can ultimately bring about effects that run counter to its aim or to the values that it is supposed to uphold. This can happen in two different ways. On the one hand, it can happen if the theory requires the individual agent to do something by virtue of which she will end up in a similar or worse position than the one she is precisely trying to remedy. On the other hand, the principle can be self-defeating if it negatively affects the wider realisation of the aim or value that it should promote. In other words, a principle is theoretically overdemanding if by pursuing it the agent herself risks falling into the very same situation that she is aiming to fix and/or if by pursuing it the agent makes it even less likely that the general outcome that is being sought is going to be achieved.[15]

When it comes to the principle of necessity, one might object that exercising it will turn out to be self-defeating for the claimant in the following sense: if what may be claimed are only the immediate means for subsistence, then the person will have to keep exercising her right again, and again, and again, trapped in her present situation and never exiting her chronically deprived state.[16] In chapter 5, however, I said that the person may also claim more than what is needed to barely survive the day if the owners of the targeted property agree to the taking, or if the resources targeted are not centrally related to the life-plans of the owner in question. Moreover, it also has to be reminded that claims of necessity for immediate subsistence made by random, disorganised individuals usually have the potential to turn into the claims of organised social movements, with the ability to make more ambitious, long-term demands, as exemplified by the Chilean *callamperos* and the Brazilian Movement of Rural Landless Workers. In sum, the objection that the practice of the right of necessity might be self-defeating for the individual claimants is not fully warranted.

Still, one might object that allowing for the exercise of the right of necessity as a means of fulfilling the right to subsistence of some is an obstacle rather than an aid for the fulfilment of the right to subsistence of all. I call this the *Remedy Worse Than the Disease* objection and formulate it next.

A Remedy Worse Than the Disease?

The question is this: What would actually happen in the world as we know it if we allowed the rule that the needy simply help themselves to the resources they require?

Instead of contributing towards the achievement of a minimally fair social structure where the basic right to subsistence of everyone is guaranteed, it seems that the disorganised and disorderly exercise of this right would run counter to what should be its ultimate goal. Even if one permits small takings to begin with, this would probably lead over time to a general breakdown of law and order: small takings would lead to larger ones; people with resources would protect them with greater and greater zeal; struggles over property would be increasingly violent; there would be a general feeling of insecurity and increased class division, with the well-off living and investing in ever more shielded and well-protected zones, and the worse-off suffering more repression and marginalisation[17]; there might even be a huge disincentive to produce and to accumulate property, so as not to attract potential claimants. This would end up severely damaging everyone's lives, and especially those whom the principle is purportedly trying to protect! Instead, it is only through firm enforcement of property rights, which give security to people, and a predictable economic and social background against which they can carry out their life-plans and projects, that chronic deprivation can come to an end.

Furthermore, if one lives in a society that looks like Underland (i.e., if one lives in a society where the basic rights of some remain chronically unfulfiled), there are good reasons to fear the untrammelled exercise of this moral prerogative, especially if one stands on the side of the potential duty-bearers rather than on the side of the potential claimants. It should also be noted that the exercise of this right by the deprived might have bad consequences for the latter, too, by perpetuating the vicious circle of poverty (as suggested in chapter 5) instead of giving a definitive solution to it—which is what the needy should be ultimately striving for. In sum, justifying the exercise of this right in situations where the claimants are not contingently but permanently deprived would have noxious effects for society at large and for the individuals affected on both sides, the objection would conclude.

This objection merits careful scrutiny. The first thing to say is the following: to accept the exercise of the right of necessity by the very deprived within a society that has not secured for all its members those material resources needed for self-preservation is not to hope for the societal order to break down into pieces. Rather, it is a reason to put into question those institutions and processes that prevent individuals from satisfying their basic right to subsistence, acknowledging at the same time that the latter have no duty to abstain from all action while this is happening. Moreover, to endorse the exercise of the right of necessity by those who invoke indigence as a justification is not to think that letting this moral prerogative be freely exercised by the needy is the final solution to their problems. Far from it—it is a reminder of the moral limitations that any reasonable property system must have, as well as a reminder that, as members of that system, each of us holds some minimal rights against, and bears some minimal duties to, each other. As Pufendorf aptly put it, a system that does not provide access to the means of subsistence to all its members cannot except itself from accepting the exercise of the right of necessity by the deprived. Doing so would be unreasonable, '[s]ince to throw off the love and care of ourselves is justly ranked amongst impossible attempts; or however amongst such as surpass the common strength of men's souls'.[18] Political stability and the security of some (even if the vast majority, self-designated as *society at large*) should not come at the cost of the lives of others. *Noxious effects*, in short, are those brought about by a system that puts people in a position such that they may permissibly claim necessity because they are chronically deprived; attributing to the latter the occurrence of the former is to put matters upside down.

Put differently, no one disagrees that the fairest and most efficient way to eradicate global poverty is via institutional change that is duly enforced. However, the question remains of what those who are needy *now* are supposed to do while these institutional reforms are put in place, if they ever are. So, what does the objector propose to say to those who remain in a chronically deprived state and whose only realistic means to satisfy their needs is the exercise of this right?

By denying the exercise of this right to the chronically deprived for the sake of keeping the social order, this objection puts the burden on those who should not bear it. If a person is needy, to the extent that he is not able to satisfy his basic needs, what is overdemanding is to require *him* to refrain from action, for the sake of keeping the state of affairs intact. And if it is the case that those who act on the right of necessity appeal to violent means (legitimately or not), then this should be a further reason to reconsider current arrangements. The mere fact that the question of the legitimacy of violence plausibly arises in such cases suggests this much.

Moreover, I have contended that the primary goal of the right of necessity is to satisfy the immediate needs of individuals, but I have also suggested that one of its possible and desirable indirect effects is the creation of organised and coordinated social and political movements making stronger and longer-term demands. This is the place to add that another possible and desirable indirect effect of accepting the exercise of this right could be to once and for all set in motion those who have so far been invested almost exclusively as the agents of change—the haves—but who have so far systematically failed to react to the call. Either for fear or (preferably) for fellow-feeling, allowing for the exercise of this right might serve as a spur for them to take steps towards the universal fulfilment of the basic right to subsistence. This is an empirical claim, to be sure, but it is no more empirical than saying that integrating this principle into cosmopolitan morality would have devastating effects, and it is at least doubtful that the latter provides reliable enough evidence to debunk the former.

A Strange Disconnect

'But the elephant is still in the room!', some might object here: it concerns the strange disconnect between the claimants and those who are ultimately responsible for their plight, or for the plight of those in a similar situation. By not discriminating between targets of appropriations, the principle of necessity might thus leave totally off the hook those directly involved in the unfulfilment of the basic needs of many, while potentially overburdening not only those who are not directly related to their plight but also those who might be taking positive steps to meet others' subsistence needs—for example, by actively participating in grassroots movements, through political involvement and action, via voluntary transfers to NGOs working on this front, and so on and so forth. The right of necessity turns out to be self-defeating, in this case, by leaving untouched those who are responsible for the unfair state of affairs that is trying to be remedied.

My response to this is that the ideal in a non-ideal world like ours would surely be to link, via the right of necessity, those who live chronically deprived lives and those who can be safely recognised as bearing primary responsibility for their deprivation. One could thus add a third tier to the recommendation suggested above, regarding the desirable profile of the owners of the targeted resources: that 'the agent should try insofar as possible to target those who, given the available evidence, it is reasonable to believe are directly responsible for his unfulfiled subsistence rights'. In the world as it is, however, leaving to the needy the task of correcting injustice by taking the resources of those responsible for their plight has a few complications, to say the least. For one thing, it might be very difficult to signal those directly responsible for one's plight, and, even if it were, it might be very costly or simply impossible to target them. More important, however, this objection relies on a notion of responsibility that is too narrow and, ultimately, inadequate for the task at hand. Without denying that there might be morally liable agents when it comes to the plight of the needy, one of the underlying assumptions of this project has been that a complex mesh of moral connections emerged as a result of partaking in a shared global economy, and that the responsibilities thence created have a diffuse, rather than well-delineated, quality.[19] Instead of singling out those directly responsible for their plight, those exercising the right of necessity single out an institutional system that allows some of its members to fall beneath minimally acceptable material thresholds. Even if by so doing they do not contribute to diminish unfairness, this should not count as a reason against their actions but—to reiterate—as a reason to strive for a global structure where serious deficits of basic human rights do not occur.

CONCLUDING REMARKS

Having accepted that the exercise of the right of necessity by the chronically deprived might create unwelcome consequences for potential duty-bearers and bring about unfair results, this chapter examined various reasons as to why, in spite of them, this moral principle ought to be upheld.

In the last chapter, I attend to the worry that theoretically empowering the needy is of little use if they are unable to claim their right in practice. I also flag three issues to be further explored if the right of necessity is integrated into moral cosmopolitanism.

NOTES

1. This term is used by Henry Shue in his book *Basic Rights*, 111.

2. On the contrary, the legal implications of justifying the exercise of the right of necessity in cases of chronic deprivation have been examined *in extenso*. See, for example, Tadros, 'Poverty and Criminal Responsibility', and Waldron, 'Why Indigence Is Not a Justification'.

3. Heilinger, 'Moral Demandingness', 195–99. I say *loosely*, because along the way I make additions and changes to each of Heilinger's original categories.

4. Heilinger subsumes epistemic overdemandingness under *technical overdemandingness*, which also includes the impossibility to *realise* a given moral principle. See Heilinger, 'Moral Demandingness', 197.

5. Samaritan duties are also vulnerable to this epistemic challenge: by accepting their existence, some might argue, many could start pretending to be in an emergency situation, just to get potential aiders to fall into their trap. Covert criminals, for example, could plead for help just to rip off innocent passersby, and covert thieves could request off-guard drivers to lend them their car in order to drive their 'seriously injured' accomplice to the hospital, never to be seen again. Yet no one seems to invoke this potential moral hazard as a reason to reject Samaritan duties.

6. The psychological difficulty that arises when moral principles require us to act in ways that are alien to our moral upbringing is absent in Heilinger's account. I take it from Michael Phillips, 'Reflections on the Transition from Ideal to Non-Ideal Theory', *Noûs* 19, 4 (1985): 558.

7. Might the principle of necessity be psychologically overdemanding even in a world in which the right to subsistence under normal circumstances is universally respected, protected and fulfiled? To bring back the imagined country of Overland, one might tailor-make a case where, by having his mountain hut iteratively targeted by stranded hikers, the hut owner's material well-being undergoes a sharp decline to the point where he ends up just above the minimally acceptable subsistence threshold. A principle that allows this to happen, the objection would go, is psychologically too taxing for potential duty-bearers. I accept that, however unlikely, this is indeed a possible outcome of fulfilling the principle of necessity—an unwelcome one to say the least. But all moral principles are subject to undesirable conclusions when taken to the extreme. In this sense, I am content to bite the bullet and accept that this is a problematic implication, but one that should not distract us from the main aim that the right of necessity promises to accomplish most of the time—that is, the satisfaction of the basic needs of individuals who have no other means to resort to.

8. For two very different sources of inspiration, see Richard Rorty, *Contingency, Irony, and Solidarity* (Cambridge: Cambridge University Press, 1989), and Adam Smith, *The Theory of Moral Sentiments*, in *The Glasgow Edition of the Works and Correspondence of Adam Smith*, ed. A. L. Macfie and D. D. Raphael, vol. 1 (Indianapolis: Liberty Fund, 1982).

9. Heilinger, 'Moral Demandingness', 198.

10. Different principles of what morality demands under conditions of general non-compliance are meticulously elaborated, among others, by Cullity, *The Moral Demands of Affluence*; Hooker, *Ideal Code, Real World*; and Murphy, 'The Demands of Beneficence'.

11. I thank Gillian Brock for suggesting the slum example above, and for proposing this clause.

12. Pufendorf, *The Law of Nature and Nations (DJN)* II.VI.6, 209.

13. How about targeting those who are responsible for the plight of the needy? Shouldn't they be the obvious first choice? I address this question below.

14. Once again, an analogy can be drawn between the duties of non-interference that correlate to the right of necessity and Samaritan duties. Imagine that, by helping someone in need on the side of the road, a person loses her car, which is indispensable for her job. As a result of fulfilling her Samaritan duty, she is left with no car and unemployed. These considerations should not exempt the person from her duty to aid the needy on the spot, but this does not preclude our affirming with equal force that she should somehow be compensated for offering aid at such high cost for herself.

15. The idea of a moral principle being self-defeating for the realisation of its wider ideal is developed by Phillips in 'Reflections on the Transition from Ideal to Non-Ideal Theory', 558–61.

16. The question whether the principle of necessity might be self-defeating for those bearing the immediate duties was answered in the last section, on psychological over-demandingness.

17. During holidays, moreover, propertied classes would probably follow Frances Kamm's recommendation, that '[i]f I want to have a quiet vacation, intuitively I may permissibly avoid going to places where I am likely to have an obligation to aid those near me': Frances Kamm, 'Faminine Ethics: The Problem of Distance in Morality and Singer's Ethical Theory', in *Singer and His Critics*, ed. Dale Jamieson (Oxford: Blackwell, 1999), 184.

18. Pufendorf, *DJN* II.VI.2, 203.

19. As mentioned at the outset, the model of shared responsibility that I have in mind here is that proposed by Iris Marion Young in 'Responsibility and Global Justice'.

SEVEN

The Right of Necessity within Moral Cosmopolitanism

I have argued so far that, while ideally confined to cases of one-off emergencies, the exercise of the right of necessity should also be accepted among the chronically deprived, under a global economic order where thousands have their subsistence needs unmet and have no other means to get out of their plight. Whereas this might admittedly disrupt the current state of affairs, I suggested in the last chapter that this disruption ought to be welcome so long as it results in the fulfilment of the basic right to subsistence of all and not just some. In what follows, I address a different worry, which might be stated thus: What is the point of upholding the moral permissibility of this right, when in the real world the chances for many (if not the majority) of the needy to actually exercise it are slim? Put differently, what is the point of *theoretically* empowering the needy when many of them remain *practically* powerless?[1] In concluding, I flag some issues that remain to be explored if this principle is endorsed by moral cosmopolitanism.

THEORETICALLY EMPOWERED, PRACTICALLY POWERLESS?

There is a proverb that says, 'If you want to go fast, go alone. If you want to go far, go together'. Applied to the topic under discussion, some might say that the right of necessity allows claimants at best to satisfy their needs *fast*. Far-reaching demands directed at satisfying one's basic right to subsistence on a stable, long-lasting basis, on the contrary, can only be achieved by acting together. Furthermore, it is not only that acting solo is not the most efficient way to get one's demands fulfiled but also that in the real world many people (maybe the majority) who are in such a position that they may permissibly claim necessity are practically incapacitated from so doing. Granting them such a right in paper, in this context, will have little or no impact in real life if they are actually prevented from exercising it.

My response to this is threefold. First, recognising that the chronically deprived have this individual right under circumstances where property rules would be irrational for them to follow and unreasonable for others to demand is a reminder that morally permissible claims may express themselves in a variety of ways—even if some of these ways are explicitly ruled out by the institutional order and, not uncommonly, by the very people theorising about them. As suggested in chapter 4, a hermeneutical injustice against the needy takes place when morally permissible claims are constrained to speech acts like demanding, shouting, protesting, and complaining, thus foreclosing the possibility to resort to physical acts like pickpocketing, pilfering, squatting, and occupying unused land.[2] If these ways of claiming necessity become accepted and acceptable, however, we might have to concede that, after all, in the real world this right is already exercised by millions on a daily basis.

Having said this, a second point to make is that it seems empirically incontestable that the best way for potential claimants to have their basic rights fulfiled is not by acting on their own but by organising themselves in larger social movements with the capacity to make longer-term demands. If this is the objection against theoretically upholding the right of necessity, however, it misfires. In fact, even though its primary goal is to secure the individual's short-term self-preservation, I have repeatedly stressed that the right of necessity can well serve as a normative cornerstone wherefrom these other collective rights should spring. Poor-led movements and movements of resistance could thus be justified as an obvious extension of it—as has in fact happened in many cases. The idea that the exercise of the individual right of necessity of their members lies at the origin of these movements has been invoked (even if not using this terminology) by groups as diverse as the Chilean *callamperos* and the Brazilian MST; the Bolivian *Coordinadora para la Defensa del Agua y de la Vida*; and squatters' organisations from Nepal, South Africa, Kenya and Turkey.[3]

Third and finally, by putting an emphasis on the existence of the right of necessity for the chronically deprived within our global society, an important aim is to entice cosmopolitan theorists to review and remap the normative landscape by incorporating this moral prerogative and the different kinds of duties that follow from it: immediate, specific duties not to interfere with the claimants' actions on the spot; mediate, general duties not to interfere by making resources inaccessible to those who may permissibly claim them; and, most important, final duties not to create and/or uphold conditions under which people may permissibly claim necessity while being at the same time practically incapacitated from doing it, or—positively stated—duties to create conditions under which the exercise of right of necessity by the chronically deprived eventually disappears. Compensatory duties towards those who have complied with their immediate and mediate duties of non-interference towards the needy are yet a fourth category that remains to be expounded and developed.

THREE ISSUES TO BE FURTHER EXPLORED

'Necessity knows no law', said Seneca. Does it know any boundaries? Illegal immigration is one topic that I have not mentioned in this book, but to which attention should naturally flow if the right of necessity is incorporated within a cosmopolitan morality. Assuming, as I have, that there is one global economic order that affects our life-prospects and connects us through a complex mesh of interrelations and interdependence (which generates, in turn, particular rights and duties), then respect for borders ought to be subsidiary to the fulfilment of one's basic right to subsistence. The permission to take, use and/or occupy someone else's property could thus be reinterpreted as a permission to take, use and/or occupy someone else's *territory*. I cannot develop here the wide range of implications of this view, but let me just point out two of them. First, it should be acknowledged that many who are currently labelled as *economic migrants* (namely, people who choose to leave their countries in order to improve their living standards and financial prospects) are doing this out of necessity, as a last resort to escape oppressive poverty. Second, many *environmental migrants* (i.e., people who leave their homes due to sudden or long-term environmental changes that affect their livelihoods) should also be understood as exercising their right of necessity rather than as merely opting for a more comfortable place to live. This reconceptualisation ought to lead to a corresponding shift in the way in which both categories of people are currently treated by immigrant-receiving countries (which many times deport them rather than accept them), as well as to a re-evaluation of the compensatory duties that third countries may owe to those bearing their immediate and mediate duties of non-interference towards these kinds of claimants.[4]

A second issue to be explored regards the implications of understanding the right of necessity as transitive—namely, as claimable by others on one's behalf. This point is especially relevant if one bears in mind that many who may permissibly claim it are unable to actually do it. At the individual level, this should translate into a tighter collaboration between the needy and those who, in more privileged positions, are willing to comply with their duties towards them. Here the role of academics and public intellectuals comes into the picture. As stressed time and again, whereas so far most of the discussion has been carried out in an abstract and detached manner, in terms of what *we* ought to do for *them*, those thinking about global poverty and moral cosmopolitanism should drop these distinctions and adopt a framework where *we* and *they* are replaced by *us* (something that can only be achieved by *working with* them rather than *thinking about* them[5]). At the collective level, meanwhile, poor-led movements and resistance movements acting as representatives of the needy should be recognised as the clearest embodiment of the transitivity of this right.

A third issue that remains to be explored concerns questioning what is perhaps the most controversial assumption of this book; to wit, that property arrangements (and the institutional system built around them) *can* in fact improve the lot of everyone. Whereas for optimistic justice and assistance cosmopolitans this is an achievable goal so long as some tinkering is done around the edges, for critics of the current neoliberal market economy and its associated legal corpus nothing less than a whole and profound structural change will do.[6] As already explained, by not choosing to call this assumption into question, my strategy has been to show that even if one believes that an institutional system where property rules are abode with and firmly enforced is the safest recipe to guarantee the satisfaction of the basic rights of all members of society, one must accept the right of necessity as a built-in limitation. To turn the right of necessity in nothing but an oddity would thus be the goal to be achieved. Closer examination to the variety of contexts in which the right of necessity is triggered today might lead one to think, however, that the existence of people who may permissibly claim necessity because they are chronically deprived is never to become exceptional but is rather an embedded feature of the global economic order as we know it. If this were the case, the normative importance of the right of necessity would become—if anything—more salient, by serving as a criterion with which to evaluate the reasonableness of the institutional structures and processes that ought to replace the current ones.

NOTES

1. I thank Michael Neu for prompting me to address this concern.

2. I am obviously not defending these actions as a general rule, but saying that many of them may constitute a legitimate exercise of the right of necessity, so that their moral permissibility should be examined case by case.

3. See Garcés, *Tomando su sitio*; Meszaros, 'Taking the Land into Their Hands'; Baer, 'From Water Wars to Water Rights'; Masako Tanaka, 'From Confrontation to Collaboration: A Decade in the Work of the Squatters' Movement in Nepal', *Environment and Urbanization* 21, 1 (2009); and Robert Neuwirth, 'Squatters and the Cities of Tomorrow', *City* 11, 1 (2007).

4. See, for example, Greece's demand that the rest of the European Union respond more effectively to the influx of refugees arriving on the former's coasts. In the first two months of 2016, Greece had already received 102,547 arrivals: 'Mediterranean Migrant, Refugee Arrivals Top 100,000', International Organization for Migration, ac-

cessed February 23, 2015, http://www.iom.int/news/mediterranean-migrant-refugee-arrivals-top-100000.

5. For a successful example of this willingness to learn and to theorise starting from the evidence, see the work of economists Abhijit V. Banerjee and Esther Duflo, *Poor Economics: A Radical Rethinking of the Way to Fight Global Poverty* (New York: Public Affairs, 2011).

6. See, among many other voices, Garry Leech, *Capitalism: A Structural Genocide* (London: Zed Books, 2012); Richard, 'A Theology of Life'; and Scott Veitch, *Law and Irresponsibility: On the Legitimation of Human Suffering* (Abingdon: Routledge, 2007).

Bibliography

Aquinas, Thomas. *Aquinas Ethicus*. Edited by Joseph Rickaby. Vol. 2. London: Burns and Oats, 1892.
Aquinas, Thomas. *Summa Theologica*. Translated by Fathers of the English Dominican Province. 2nd and rev. ed., 1920. Accessed July 17, 2015. http://www.newadvent.org/summa/.
Aristotle. *Nicomachean Ethics*. Edited by Jonathan Barnes. *The Complete Works of Aristotle, Bollingen Series LXXI-2*. Vol. 2. Princeton, NJ: Princeton University Press, 1984.
Ashford, Elizabeth. 'Duties Imposed by the Human Right to Basic Necessities'. In *Freedom from Poverty as a Human Right*, edited by Thomas Pogge, 183–218. Oxford: Oxford University Press, 2007.
Baer, Madeline. 'From Water Wars to Water Rights: Implementing the Human Right to Water in Bolivia'. *Journal of Human Rights* 14, 3 (2015): 353–76.
Banerjee, Abhijit V., and Esther Duflo. *Poor Economics: A Radical Rethinking of the Way to Fight Global Poverty*. New York: Public Affairs, 2011.
Barry, Christian, and Gerhard Øverland. 'The Feasible Alternatives Thesis: Kicking Away the Livelihoods of the Global Poor?' *Politics Philosophy Economics* 11, 1 (2012): 97–119.
Barry, Christian, and Gerhard Øverland. 'The Implications of Failing to Assist'. *Social Theory and Practice* 40, 4 (2014): 570–90.
Benson, Robert L., and Giles Constable. *Renaissance and Renewal in the Twelfth Century*. Cambridge, MA: Harvard University Press, 1982.
Bonavitta, Paola, and Marcos Servín Valencia. 'Las ciudades de los excluidos en una Latinoamérica posmoderna'. *Kairos: Revista de Temas Sociales* 29 (2012): 1–12.
Brock, Gillian. 'Is Redistribution to Help the Needy Unjust?' *Analysis* 55, 1 (1995): 50–60.
Brudner, Alan. 'A Theory of Necessity'. *Oxford Journal of Legal Studies* 7, 3 (1987): 339–68.
Buckle, Stephen. *Natural Law and the Theory of Property: Grotius to Hume*. New York: Clarendon Press, 1991.
Butler, Patrick. 'Food Poverty: "I Was Brought Up Not to Steal. But That's How Bad It's Got"'. *Guardian*, June 24, 2013. Accessed October 15, 2015. http://www.theguardian.com/society/patrick-butler-cuts-blog/2013/jun/24/food-poverty-growth-in-shoplifting-groceries.
Campbell, Tom. 'Poverty as a Violation of Human Rights: Inhumanity or Injustice?', in *Freedom from Poverty as a Human Right*, edited by Thomas Pogge, 55–74. New York: Oxford University Press, 2007.
Caney, Simon. 'Responding to Global Injustice: On the Right of Resistance'. *Social Philosophy and Policy* 32, 1 (2015): 51–73.
Cockell, Charles. *Extraterrestrial Liberty: An Enquiry into the Nature and Causes of Tyrannical Government beyond the Earth*. Edinburgh: Shoving Leopard, 2013.
Cohen, Joshua. 'Philosophy, Social Science and Poverty'. In *Thomas Pogge and His Critics*, edited by Alison Jaggar, 18–45. Malden, MA: Polity Press, 2010.
Credit Suisse Research Institute. *Global Wealth Report 2015*. Accessed October 15, 2015. http://publications.credit-suisse.com/tasks/render/file/index.cfm?fileid=C26E3824-E868-56E0-CCA04D4BB9B9ADD5.
Cullity, Garrett. *The Moral Demands of Affluence*. New York: Clarendon Press, 2004.

Darwall, Stephen. 'Pufendorf on Morality, Sociability, and Moral Powers'. *Journal of the History of Philosophy* 50, 2 (2012): 213–38.
Davidson, Lauren. 'Shoplifting in Russia Is Soaring as the Economy Crumbles'. *Telegraph*, July 23, 2015. Accessed October 15, 2015. http://www.telegraph.co.uk/finance/economics/11759336/Shoplifting-in-Russia-is-soaring-as-the-economy-crumbles.html.
De Vattel, Emer. *The Law of Nations*. Edited by Béla Kaposy and Richard Whatmore. Indianapolis: Liberty Fund, 2008.
Deveaux, Monique. 'The Global Poor as Agents of Justice'. *Journal of Moral Philosophy* 12 (2015): 125–50.
Dressler, Joshua. 'Exegesis of the Law of Duress: Justifying the Excuse and Searching for Its Proper Limits'. *Southern California Law Review* 62 (1988): 1331–86.
Dunford, Robin. 'Human Rights and Collective Emancipation: The Politics of Food Sovereignty'. *Review of International Studies* 41, 2 (2014): 239–61.
Eide, Asbjørn. 'Article 25'. In *The Universal Declaration of Human Rights: A Commentary*, edited by Asbjørn Eide and T. Swinehart, 385–403. Oslo: Scandinavian University Press, 1993.
Fabre, Cécile. *Cosmopolitan War*. Oxford: Oxford University Press, 2012.
Feinberg, Joel. *Social Philosophy*. Englewood Cliffs, NJ: Prentice-Hall, 1973.
Feinberg, Joel. 'Voluntary Euthanasia and the Inalienable Right to Life'. *Philosophy & Public Affairs* 7, 2 (1978): 93–123.
Fleischacker, Samuel. *A Short History of Distributive Justice*. Cambridge, MA: Harvard University Press, 2004.
Fletcher, George P. 'The Individualization of Excusing Conditions'. In *Justification and Excuse in the Criminal Law*, edited by Michael Louis Corrado, 53–94. New York: Garland Publishing, 1994.
Fricker, Miranda. *Epistemic Injustice: Power and the Ethics of Knowing*. Oxford: Oxford University Press, 2007.
Garcés, Mario. *Tomando su sitio: El movimiento de pobladores de Santiago 1957–1970*. Santiago de Chile: LOM Ediciones, 2002.
Gargarella, Roberto. 'The Right of Resistance in Situations of Severe Deprivation'. In *Freedom from Poverty as a Human Right*, edited by Thomas Pogge, 359–74. New York: Oxford University Press, 2007.
Gewirth, Alan. 'Duties to Fulfill the Human Rights of the Poor'. In *Freedom from Poverty as a Human Right*, edited by Thomas Pogge, 219–36. New York: Oxford University Press, 2007.
Gewirth, Alan. 'The Justification of Morality'. *Philosophical Studies* 53, 2 (1988): 245–62.
Gilabert, Pablo. 'The Duty to Eradicate Global Poverty: Positive or Negative?' *Ethical Theory and Moral Practice* 7, 5 (2004): 537–50.
Gould, Carol C. 'Coercion, Care, and Corporations: Omissions and Commissions in Thomas Pogge's Political Philosophy'. *Journal of Global Ethics* 3, 3 (2007): 381–93.
Griffin, James. *On Human Rights*. Oxford: Oxford University Press, 2008.
Groh-Samberg, Olaf. 'Increasing Persistent Poverty in Germany'. *Weekly Report*, German Institute for Economic Research (DIW), Berlin, vol. 3, 4 (2007): 21–26.
Grotius, Hugo. *The Law of War and Peace*. Translated by F. W. Kelsey. Washington, DC: Carnegie Institution, 1913.
Haakonssen, Knud. 'Hugo Grotius and the History of Political Thought'. *Political Theory* 13, 2 (1985): 239–65.
Harvey, David. 'The Culture of Poverty: An Ideological Analysis'. *Sociological Perspectives* 39, 4 (1996): 465–95.
Heilinger, Jan-Christoph. 'The Moral Demandingness of Socioeconomic Human Rights'. In *The Philosophy of Human Rights Contemporary Controversies*, edited by Jan-Christoph Heilinger and Gerhard Ernst, 185–208. Berlin: De Gruyter, 2012.
Hobbes, Thomas. *Leviathan*, vol. 2, edited by Noel Malcolm. Oxford: Clarendon Press, 2012.

Hohfeld, Wesley Newcomb. 'Some Fundamental Legal Conceptions as Applied in Judicial Reasoning'. *Yale Law Journal* 23, 1 (1913): 16–59.

Holmbäck, Åke, and Elias Wessén, eds. *Svenska Landskapslagar: Tolkade Och Förklarade För Nutidens Svenskar.* Vol. 3. Uppsala: Hugo Gebers Förlag, 1940.

Hooker, Brad. *Ideal Code, Real World: A Rule-Consequentialist Theory of Morality.* Oxford and New York: Clarendon Press, 2000.

Hutcheson, Francis. *A Short Introduction to Moral Philosophy.* Edited by Luigi Turco. Indianapolis: Liberty Fund, 2007.

Hutcheson, Francis. *A System of Moral Philosophy in Three Books.* Edited by William Leechman. Glasgow: Printed by R. and A. Foulis, 1755.

Institute for Global Labor and Human Rights and Federation of Independent Associations and Unions of El Salvador. 'Dressing Babies in Sweatshop Clothing: Dallas Cowboys, Ohio State and a Creepy Business'. Joint Report, October 2011. Accessed January 22, 2016. http://www.globallabourrights.org/reports/document/1110-IGLHR-DressingBabiesInSweatshopClothing-StyleAvenue-1.pdf.

Kamm, Frances. 'Faminine Ethics: The Problem of Distance in Morality and Singer's Ethical Theory'. In *Singer and His Critics,* edited by Dale Jamieson, 162–208. Oxford: Blackwell, 1999.

Kilcullen, John. 'The Origin of Property: Ockham, Grotius, Pufendorf, and Some Others'. 1995. Accessed August 10, 2015. http://www.mq.edu.au/about_us/faculties_and_departments/faculty_of_arts/mhpir/staff/staff-politics_and_international_relations/john_kilcullen/the_origin_of_property_ockham_grotius_pufendorf_and_some_others/.

Klimchuk, Dennis. 'Property and Necessity'. In *Philosophical Foundations of Property Law,* edited by James Penner and Henry Smith, 47–67. Oxford: Oxford University Press, 2013.

Krahmer, Holger, 'India's Lawless War on Intellectual Property'. *Wall Street Journal,* March 23, 2014. Accessed January 22, 2016. http://www.wsj.com/articles/SB10001424052702304679404579456672440016300/.

Leech, Garry. *Capitalism: A Structural Genocide.* London: Zed Books, 2012.

Lippert-Rasmussen, Kasper. 'Global Injustice and Redistributive Wars'. *Law, Ethics and Philosophy* 1, 1 (2013): 65–86.

Locke, John. *Two Treatises of Government.* Edited by Peter Laslett. Cambridge: Cambridge University Press, 1988.

Luban, David. 'Just War and Human Rights'. *Philosophy & Public Affairs* 9, 2 (1980): 160–81.

MacAskill, William. *Doing Good Better: How Effective Altruism Can Help You Make a Difference.* London: Gotham, 2015.

MacIntyre, Alasdair. *Whose Justice? Which Rationality?* Notre Dame: University of Notre Dame Press, 1988.

Mäkinen, Virpi. 'Individual Natural Rights in the Discussion on Franciscan Poverty'. *Studia Theologica* 53 (1999): 50–57.

Mäkinen, Virpi. 'Rights and Duties in Late Scholastic Discussion on Extreme Necessity'. In *Transformations in Medieval and Early Modern Rights Discourse,* edited by Virpi Mäkinen and Petter Korkman, 37–62. Dordrecht: Springer, 2006.

Mancilla, Alejandra. 'Samuel Pufendorf and the Right of Necessity'. *Aporia* 3 (2012): 47–64.

Matthaeus, Antonius. *Of Crimes: A Commentary on Books XLVII and XLVIII of the Digest.* Edited by M. L. Hewett. Cape Town: Juta, 1987.

Mautner, Thomas. 'Introduction: A Lawless Natural Law?' to Karl Olivecrona, 'Two Levels of Natural Law Thinking'. Translated by Thomas Mautner, 197–208, *Jurisprudence* 1, 2 (2010): 197–224.

Mautner, Thomas. 'Pufendorf and 18th-Century Scottish Philosophy'. *Samuel von Pufendorf 1632–1982. Ett Rättshistoriskt Symposium i Lund.* Lund: Bloms Boktryckeri AB, 1982.

Meszaros, George. 'Taking the Land into Their Hands: The Landless Workers' Movement and the Brazilian State'. *Journal of Law and Society* 27, 4 (2000): 517–41.
Miller, Richard W. 'Beneficence, Duty and Distance'. *Philosophy and Public Affairs* 32, 4 (2004): 357–83.
Model Penal Code Annotated (Proposed Official Draft 1962). Criminal Law Web. Accessed January 7, 2016. http://www.law-lib.utoronto.ca/bclc/crimweb/web1/mpc/mpc.html#fn1.
Murphy, Liam B. 'The Demands of Beneficence'. *Philosophy and Public Affairs* 22, 4 (1993): 267–92.
Mutisya, Emmanuel, and Masaru Yarime. 'Understanding the Grassroots Dynamics of Slums in Nairobi: The Dilemma of Kibera Informal Settlements'. *International Transaction Journal of Engineering, Management, & Applied Sciences & Technologies* 2, 2 (2011). Accessed December 10, 2015, http://tuengr.com/V02/197-213.pdf.
Narveson, Jan. 'Property and Rights'. *Social Philosophy and Policy* 27, 1 (2010): 101–34.
Neuwirth, Robert. 'Squatters and the Cities of Tomorrow'. *City* 11, 1 (2007): 71–80.
Nickel, James. *Making Sense of Human Rights*. 2nd ed. Malden, MA: Blackwell, 2007. Originally published 1987.
Olivecrona, Karl. 'Appropriation in the State of Nature: Locke on the Origin of Property'. *Journal of the History of Ideas* 35, 2 (1974): 211–30.
Olivecrona, Karl. 'The Two Levels in Natural Law Thinking'. Translated with an introduction by Thomas Mautner. *Jurisprudence* 2 (2010): 197–224.
O'Neill, Onora. *Bounds of Justice*. Cambridge: Cambridge University Press, 2000.
O'Neill, Onora. 'The Dark Side of Human Rights'. *International Affairs* 81, 2 (2005): 427–39.
O'Neill, Onora. 'Rights, Obligations and Needs'. In *Necessary Goods*, edited by Gillian Brock, 95–112. Lanham, MD: Rowman & Littlefield, 1998. Originally published in *Logos* 6 (1985): 29–47.
Organisation for Economic Co-operation and Development. *Divided We Stand: Why Inequality Keeps Rising*. 2011. Accessed October 15, 2015. http://www.keepeek.com/Digital-Asset-Management/oecd/social-issues-migration-health/the-causes-of-growing-inequalities-in-oecd-countries_9789264119536-en.
Øverland, Gerhard. 'Forced Assistance'. *Law and Philosophy* 28, 2 (2009): 203–32.
Øverland, Gerhard. 'Just Adjustments'. In *Treating Others*, 113–94. Oslo: Unipub, 2002.
Øverland, Gerhard. 'The Right to Do Wrong'. *Law and Philosophy* 26, 4 (2007): 377–404.
Patten, Alan. 'Should We Stop Thinking about Poverty in Terms of Helping the Poor?' *Ethics & International Affairs* 19, 1 (2005): 19–27.
Phillips, Michael. 'Reflections on the Transition from Ideal to Non-Ideal Theory'. *Noûs* 19, 4 (1985): 551–70.
Pogge, Thomas. *Politics as Usual*. Cambridge: Polity Press, 2010.
Pogge, Thomas. 'Poverty and Violence'. *Law Ethics and Philosophy* 1 (2013): 87–111.
Pogge, Thomas. *World Poverty and Human Rights: Cosmopolitan Responsibilities and Reforms*. 2nd ed. Malden, MA: Polity Press, 2008. Originally published 2002.
Pufendorf, Samuel. *Of the Law of Nature and Nations*. Translated by Basil Kennet, with annotations by Jean de Barbeyrac. 8 volumes. 4th ed. London: Printed for J. Walthoe, 1729.
Pufendorf, Samuel. *Two Books of the Elements of Universal Jurisprudence*. Edited by Thomas Behme, translated by William Abbott Oldfather. Indianapolis: Liberty Fund, 2009.
Pufendorf, Samuel. *The Whole Duty of Man*. Edited by Ian Hunter and David Saunders. Indianapolis: Liberty Fund, 2003.
Rancière, Jacques. 'Who Is the Subject of the Rights of Man?' In *Dissensus: On Politics and Aesthetics*, 70–83. London: Bloomsbury, 2010.
Rawls, John. *Political Liberalism*. Expanded ed. New York: Columbia University Press, 2005. Originally published 1993.

Richard, Pablo. 'A Theology of Life: Rebuilding Hope from the Perspective of the South'. In *Spirituality of the Third World: A Cry for Life*, edited by K. C. Abraham and Bernadette Mbuy-Beya, 92–108. Eugene, OR: Wipf and Stock, 2005.

Risse, Mathias. 'Do We Owe the Global Poor Assistance or Rectification?' *Ethics and International Affairs* 19, 1 (2005): 9–18.

Risse, Mathias. *On Global Justice*. Princeton, NJ: Princeton University Press, 2012.

Robinson, Paul H. 'Criminal Law Defenses: A Systematic Analysis'. *Columbia Law Review* 82, 2 (1982): 199–291.

Rorty, Richard. *Contingency, Irony, and Solidarity*. Cambridge: Cambridge University Press, 1989.

Saastamoinen, Kari. 'Pufendorf on Natural Equality, Human Dignity, and Self-Esteem'. *Journal of the History of Ideas* 71, 1 (2010): 39–62.

Salinger, Tobias. 'Police Officer Who Caught Homeless Mom Stealing for Children at Walmart Buys Diapers, Wipes, Shoes for Her'. *New York Daily News*, July 11, 2015. Accessed November 30, 2015. http://www.nydailynews.com/news/crime/caught-homeless-mom-stealing-buys-diapers-article-1.2289506.

Salter, John. 'Grotius and Pufendorf on the Right of Necessity'. *History of Political Thought* 26, 2 (2005): 285–302.

Salter, John. 'Hugo Grotius: Property and Consent'. *Political Theory* 29, 4 (2001): 537–55.

Sanghera, Balihar, and Elmira Satybaldieva. 'Ethics of Property, Illegal Settlements and the Right to Subsistence'. *International Journal of Sociology and Social Policy* 32, 1/2 (2012): 96–114.

Satz, Debra. 'What Do We Owe the Global Poor?' *Ethics and International Affairs* 19, 1 (2005): 47–54.

Schneewind, Jerome. *The Invention of Autonomy: A History of Modern Moral Philosophy*. Cambridge: Cambridge University Press, 1998.

Schneewind, Jerome. 'Pufendorf's Place in the History of Ethics'. *Synthese* 72, 1 (1987): 123–55.

Shearmur, Jeremy. 'The Right to Subsistence in a "Lockean" State of Nature'. *Southern Journal of Philosophy* XXVII, 4 (1989): 561–68.

Shue, Henry. *Basic Rights: Subsistence, Affluence, and U.S. Foreign Policy*. 2nd ed. Princeton, NJ: Princeton University Press, 1996. Originally published 1980.

Simmons, A. John. *The Lockean Theory of Rights*. Princeton, NJ: Princeton University Press, 1992.

Singer, Peter. 'Famine, Affluence, and Morality'. *Philosophy and Public Affairs* 1, 3 (1972): 229–43.

Singer, Peter. *The Life You Can Save*. Melbourne: Text Publishing, 2009.

Skinner, Quentin. 'Meaning and Understanding in the History of Ideas'. *History and Theory* 8, 1 (1969): 3–53.

Smith, Adam. *An Inquiry into the Nature and Causes of the Wealth of Nations*, vol. 2. Edited by Edwin Cannan. London: Methuen & Co., 1904.

Smith, Adam. *The Theory of Moral Sentiments*. Edited by A. L. Macfie and D. D. Raphael. *The Glasgow Edition of the Works and Correspondence of Adam Smith*. Vol. 1. Indianapolis: Liberty Fund, 1982.

Steinhoff, Uwe. *On the Ethics of War and Terrorism*. Oxford: Oxford University Press, 2007.

Swanson, Scott G. 'The Medieval Foundations of John Locke's Theory of Natural Rights: Rights of Subsistence and the Principle of Extreme Necessity'. *History of Political Thought* 18, 3 (1997): 400–458.

Tadros, Victor. 'Poverty and Criminal Responsibility'. *Journal of Value Inquiry* 43 (2009): 391–413.

Tanaka, Masako. 'From Confrontation to Collaboration: A Decade in the Work of the Squatters' Movement in Nepal'. *Environment and Urbanization* 21, 1 (2009): 143–59.

Tasioulas, John. 'Taking Rights out of Human Rights'. In *Griffin on Human Rights*, edited by Roger Crisp, 9–45. Oxford: Oxford University Press, 2014.

Tavernise, Sabrina. 'Soaring Poverty Casts Spotlight on Lost Decade'. *New York Times*, September 13, 2011. Accessed October 15, 2015. http://www.nytimes.com/2011/09/14/us/14census.html?_r=0.

Taylor, Diane. 'Manchester United Stars Neville and Giggs Tell Hotel Squatters: Stay for Winter'. *Guardian*, October 19, 2015. Accessed January 22, 2015. http://www.theguardian.com/society/2015/oct/18/former-manchester-united-star-occupiers-of-hotel-winter-ryan-giggs-gary-neville.

Thomson, Judith Jarvis. *The Realm of Rights*. Cambridge, MA: Harvard University Press, 1990.

Tierney, Brian. *The Idea of Natural Rights*. Atlanta: Scholars Press, 1997.

Tierney, Brian. *Medieval Poor Law: A Sketch of Canonical Theory and Its Application in England*. Berkeley: University of California Press, 1959.

Tierney, Brian. 'Origins of Natural Rights Language: Texts and Contexts, 1150–1250'. *History of Political Thought* 10 (1989): 615–46.

Tuck, Richard. *The Rights of War and Peace: Political Thought and the International Order from Grotius to Kant*. Oxford: Oxford University Press, 1999.

Unger, Peter. *Living High and Letting Die*. New York: Oxford University Press, 1996.

United Nations. Millennium Development Goals Report 2015 (2015). Accessed October 15, 2015. http://www.un.org/millenniumgoals/2015_MDG_Report/pdf/MDG%202015%20rev%20%28July%201%29.pdf.

United Nations. Universal Declaration of Human Rights. Accessed January 12, 2016. http://www.un.org/en/universal-declaration-human-rights/.

Van Duffel, Siegfried, and Dennis Yap. 'Distributive Justice before the Eighteenth Century: The Right of Necessity'. *History of Political Thought* 32, 3 (2011): 449–64.

Veitch, Scott. *Law and Irresponsibility: On the Legitimation of Human Suffering*. Abingdon: Routledge, 2007.

Waldron, Jeremy. 'The Advantages and Difficulties of the Humean Theory of Property'. *Social Philosophy and Policy* 11 (1994): 85–123.

Waldron, Jeremy. 'A Right to Do Wrong'. *Ethics* 92, 1 (1981): 21–39.

Waldron, Jeremy. 'Why Indigence Is Not a Justification'. In *From Social Justice to Criminal Justice*, edited by Hugh Heffernan and John Kleinig, 98–113. Oxford: Oxford University Press, 2000.

Winn, Patrick. 'Here's How the Cambodians Who Stitch Your Clothes Are Routinely Abused'. *Global Post*, March 19, 2015. Accessed January 22, 2016. http://www.globalpost.com/dispatch/news/regions/asia-pacific/cambodia/150319/the-cambodians-who-stitch-your-clothes-routinely-abused-exploited.

Young, Iris Marion. 'Responsibility and Global Justice: A Social Connection Model'. *Social Philosophy and Policy* 23, 1 (2006): 102–30.

Index

air, 66, 81, 93n1
Alanus, 29
almsgiving, 41n22, 49
Ambrose of Milan, 27
Aquinas, Thomas, 16, 17, 25, 26, 27, 31, 39, 41n17, 41n22, 46; on right of necessity, 28–29, 81
Aristotle, 28–29
Ashford, Elizabeth, 79n27
assistance cosmopolitanism. *See* cosmopolitanism
Augustine, 28–29

Bangladesh, 92
Barbeyrac, Jean, 25
billionaires, 9, 20n29
Bolivia, 88, 112
Bonaventure, 29
borrowing privilege, 72
Brazil, 20n29, 88, 105, 112
Britton law book, 30
Buckle, Stephen, 48, 54

callamperos, 10, 87–88, 105, 112
Campbell, Tom, 19n12
Caney, Simon, 10–11
Carmichael, Gershom, 25
Chile, 10, 87, 105, 112
China, 20n29
Christian canon law, 16, 17, 25, 27, 29–30, 31, 39
chronic deprivation, 14, 17, 42n34, 61n36, 72, 76, 82, 87, 109n2; chronically deprived agents, 4, 6, 8, 9, 12, 16, 29–30, 39, 46, 59, 66, 71, 72, 76, 78n11, 86, 91, 95n19, 97–108, 111–114
church, 31, 49; Fathers, 27
Cicero, 32, 38, 47
civil law, 13, 30, 31, 39

civil society, 28, 32, 35, 39, 47, 59
clothing, 27, 49, 53, 66, 77n1, 81
Cockell, Charles, 93n1
common law, 13, 30, 31, 39, 40n5
Coordinadora para la Defensa del Agua y de la Vida, 88, 112
cosmopolitanism: assistance, 2–3, 11–12, 13, 18n4, 27; justice, 2, 3, 8, 10–11, 18n4, 19n7, 27, 72, 73; moral, 1–2, 14, 15, 26, 66, 70, 72–76, 86, 92, 93, 98, 103, 104, 107, 108, 111–114; war, 8–10, 11
criminal law, 13, 78n10, 86
Curtius, 38

de Clavasio, Angelo, 28
Denning, Lord, 21n49
De Vattel, Emer, 16, 25
Deveaux, Monique, 10
de Vitoria, Francisco, 25
Dominicans, 28
duties: allocation of, 6, 74, 75, 102–104; of assistance, 2–3, 11–13, 25, 27, 48; of avoidance, protection and aid, 5, 20n23, 69; compensatory, 61n36, 95n19, 102–104, 109n14, 113; final, 5–6, 13, 18, 76, 86, 87, 97, 99, 103–104, 112; of non-interference, immediate, 5, 18, 61n36, 75, 86–87, 93, 97, 100, 102–104, 112, 113; of non-interference, mediate, 5, 18, 61n36, 86–87, 97, 102–104, 112, 113; of restitution, 28, 30, 38–39, 40, 52, 53, 54, 59, 61n36, 95n19; Samaritan, 75, 109n5, 109n14. *See also* Pufendorf, Samuel

economic migrants, 113
Eide, Asbjørn, 69

Index

emergencies, 4, 30, 42n34, 59, 70–71, 82, 87, 94n11, 109n5, 111
energy, 66, 81
environmental migrants, 113
epistemic limitations, 56, 91. *See also* overdemandingness
equally important moral interests condition. *See* right of necessity
equity. *See* natural equity
European Union, 114n4
evangelical denunciation, 31

Fabre, Cécile, 8–9, 10
favourable conditions, 14, 16, 26
Feinberg, Joel, 21n44
Filmer, Robert, 27
Fleischacker, Samuel, 42n28
food, 1, 10, 12, 28, 29, 38, 49, 51, 66, 70, 74, 77n1, 81, 82
force, use of, 8, 35, 36, 37, 38, 40, 47, 49, 51–52, 53, 58, 68, 79n19, 87–88, 95n21
forced assistance, 7, 11–13
Franciscans, 41n23
Fricker, Miranda, 74

Garcés, Mario, 87–88
Gargarella, Roberto, 10
Gewirth, Alan, 67, 79n19
Gilabert, Pablo, 19n7
global assistance. *See* cosmopolitanism
global economic order/structure, 9, 13, 14, 16, 18, 40n3, 71, 72, 73, 82, 83, 87, 108, 111, 113, 114
global justice. *See* cosmopolitanism
global poverty, 6, 9, 11, 13, 73, 74, 87, 106; debate, 5, 17, 26, 66, 72, 75–76, 91, 98, 114; statistics of, 1, 73
global taxation, 3, 19n12
God, 27, 29, 31, 41n18, 41n23, 42n29, 45
Greece, 114n4
Griffin, James, 66–67
Grotius, Hugo, 16, 17, 30, 45, 46, 47, 51, 54, 57, 67, 85; on common use rights, 32–37, 40, 58, 59; on property arrangements/rights, 32–34, 37, 40, 68, 70; on right of necessity, 17, 25–26, 31–40, 53, 81; on state of nature, 32, 34, 68, 78n7

hacktivists, 21n42
Hart, H. L. A., 43n39
healthcare/medical provisions, basic, 10, 66, 77n1, 81, 86
Heilinger, Jan-Christoph, 95n21, 98, 109n4, 109n6
hermeneutical injustice, 74, 112
hiker-in-the-storm example, 13, 17, 70–71, 76, 93n2
Hobbes, Thomas, 25, 26, 32; on right of nature, 89
Hohfeld, Wesley Newcomb, 36, 42n35; typology of rights, 4–5, 34, 39–40, 50, 81
Hostiensis, 30
Huguccio, 28
human rights, 1–4, 5, 8, 10, 19n15, 19n17, 65, 67, 72–73, 77n3, 79n19, 79n27, 100, 108; critique of, 75, 80n32. *See also* Universal Declaration of Human Rights
Hume, David. *See* property arrangements/rights
Hutcheson, Francis, 16, 25, 26, 40n5

illegal immigration, 113, 114n4
India, 20n29, 94n9

Jewish law, 49
John XXII (pope), 41n23
justice, claims of, 9, 83–84, 95n21
justice cosmopolitanism. *See* cosmopolitanism

Kamm, Frances, 110n17
Kenya, 112
Kyrgyzstan, 94n14

Lactantius, 38
landless peasants, 82, 112. *See also* Movement of Rural Landless Workers
last resort condition. *See* right of necessity
Laurentius Hispanus, 29–30
liability, 8, 9, 83, 108
liberation theology, 95n18
libertarianism, 77n6
life-plans/life-projects, 16, 83–84, 105

Lippert-Rasmussen, Kasper, 8, 20n27, 79n26
Locke, John, 16, 25, 26, 27, 41n7. *See also* property arrangements/rights
London Borough of Southwark v. Williams, 21n49
Lord Simon of Glaisdale in DPP v. Lynch, 14

MacIntyre, Alasdair, 26
manifesto rights. *See* subsistence, basic right to
Matthaeus, Antonius, II, 51
moral cosmopolitanism. *See* cosmopolitanism
moral innocence condition. *See* right of necessity
Movement of Rural Landless Workers (MST), 88, 95n16, 105, 112
multinational companies, 88

natural equity, 31, 33, 40, 51, 70
natural law, 16, 25, 28, 29, 31, 32, 34, 35, 38, 45, 47, 51, 58, 59, 60n3
needs, basic, 5–6, 9, 10, 14, 26, 43n39, 66, 71, 72, 77n6, 79n15, 84, 93n2, 96n26, 97, 104, 107, 109n7. *See also* right of necessity
Nepal, 112
Nickel, James, 67
non-compliance, 95n21, 100, 101, 103, 109n10
non-interference, claim of, 4, 5, 18, 37, 40, 81, 85, 92–93
normative agency, 66–67
Northup, Solomon, 89
Nozick, Robert, 77n6
nuclear weapons, 82, 84

Olivecrona, Karl, 35, 45
O'Neill, Onora, 5, 74, 75, 103
overdemandingness, 54, 83, 85, 97–108; epistemic, 18, 98–100, 102–103, 109n5; psychological, 18, 98, 100–104, 109n7; theoretical, 18, 90, 95n21, 98, 104–108
Overland, 70–71, 79n16, 89, 95n19, 109n7

Øverland, Gerhard, 12, 13; adjustment principle, 78n10

personhood. *See* normative agency
Phillips, Michael, 109n6, 110n15
pickpocketing, 97, 112
Podemos (political party), 84
Pogge, Thomas, 2, 3, 8, 20n27, 72–74, 75, 79n25, 87
police, 5, 7, 86, 94n10, 97
poor-led movements, 7, 10, 11, 95n18, 112, 114
Prieras, Sylvester, 28
privilege rights, 4–5, 17–18, 34–37, 40, 42n35, 43n39, 56, 58, 68, 81, 85, 92, 97. *See also* right of necessity
property arrangements/rights, 6–7, 14, 15–16, 26, 30, 41n17, 65, 68–72, 87, 88, 90, 97, 101, 105, 114; consequentialist theories of, 77n6; Humean theories of, 77n6; institution of, 32–33, 48, 114; libertarian theories of, 77n6; Lockean theories of, 77n6, 93n3; social contract theories of, 68, 69–70. *See also* Grotius, Hugo; Pufendorf, Samuel
Pufendorf, Samuel, 16, 17, 25, 35, 38, 39, 40, 41n22, 43n37, 43n39, 45, 60n2, 67, 68, 70, 85, 90, 95n19, 102, 106; on absolute and conditional or hypothetical duties, 46, 56, 57; on enforceable duty of humanity, 46, 49–50, 51–52, 58; on perfect and imperfect rights and duties, 33, 46–47, 48–49, 52, 56, 57, 58, 59, 60n31; on property arrangements/ rights, 47–58, 59, 60n24, 68, 70; on pull of self-preservation, 17, 46, 50–51, 52–57, 59; on right of necessity, 17, 26, 30, 45–59, 60n24, 81, 82; on sociability, 46, 47, 48, 55; on state of nature, 47, 68, 78n7

Rana Plaza, 92
Rancière, Jacques, 80n32
Rawls, John, 2, 79n15
Remedy Worse Than the Disease objection, 93, 105–107

resistance, 10–11, 76, 87–88, 95n18, 112, 114
resource privilege, 72
restitution. *See* duties; Grotius, Hugo
right of necessity: basic needs condition, 4, 88, 89, 93, 102; as concrete expression/manifestation of basic right to subsistence, 5, 6, 11, 16, 17, 65, 70–72, 75, 76, 77n1, 81; conditions of, 4, 18, 52–56, 59, 81, 88–92, 93, 95n19, 102; content of, 17, 81–85, 93n2; definition of, 4–5, 65, 85, 92, 97; as duty toward God, 29, 41n18, 41n23; as exceptional moral prerogative, 4, 7, 17, 26, 36, 40, 50–51, 59, 72, 76, 87, 99; equally important moral interests condition, 4, 9, 88–91, 93, 102; form of, 4–5, 17–18, 81, 85–88; last resort condition, 4, 10, 30, 37, 39, 52, 54, 88, 91–92, 93, 102; legal conception of, 13–14, 21n48–21n49, 109n2; as liberty, 4, 18, 81, 85–86, 90, 92–93, 96n23, 97; medieval conceptions of, 4, 14, 16, 25–31, 32, 39, 42n34; as mere privilege, 17, 34–37, 38, 39, 40, 84, 90, 96n23; moral innocence condition, 53, 54, 56, 61n35, 95n19; as revival of the right of common use, 17, 33, 34, 35, 36, 37, 39–40, 58; as transitive right, 12, 21n42, 30, 39, 113–114. *See also* Aquinas, Thomas; Grotius, Hugo; Pufendorf, Samuel
rights: claim, 4, 5, 17, 34–37; common use, 17, 25, 28, 43n39; to do wrong, 6; liberty, 9, 67, 74, 79n15, 84, 89, 90, 92, 97; of man, 75; welfare, 74, 75, 80n33. *See also* Grotius, Hugo; human rights; non-interference, claim of; privilege rights; property arrangements/rights; Pufendorf, Samuel; right of necessity; security, basic right to; subsistence, basic right to
Risse, Mathias, 42n30, 43n39
Rorty, Richard, 109n8

Salter, John, 34–35, 57–58
Samaritan duties. *See* duties

security, basic right to, 65, 66, 67, 77n1, 85, 92
Selden, John, 49
self-defence, 9, 65, 71
self-preservation, 3, 4, 11, 55, 65, 66, 68, 70, 72, 75, 76, 80n33, 86, 99, 106, 112. *See also* Pufendorf, Samuel
Seneca, 4, 113
shelter, 49, 66, 81, 82, 84
shoplifting. *See* theft
Shue, Henry, 20n23, 66, 69, 108n1
Simmons, A. John, 93n3
Singer, Peter, 19n16; principle of assistance, 2, 19n8, 100
slavery, 37, 43n45, 89; self-enslavement, 54–55, 92
Smith, Adam, 94n5, 109n8
sociability. *See* Pufendorf, Samuel
social connection model of responsibility, 9, 61n35, 83
social contract theories of property rights. *See* Grotius, Hugo; property arrangements/rights; Pufendorf, Samuel
social movements, 87–88, 107. *See also* poor-led movements
solidarity, 11, 55, 58, 59, 84, 85, 86, 95n18
South Africa, 112
Spain, 84
squatters, 83, 84, 86, 112. *See also* urban homeless
subsistence, 30, 32, 40, 50, 55, 59, 81, 82–83, 85, 88, 92, 93n1–93n2, 94n5, 102, 105, 107, 109n7, 111; wars, 7, 8, 20n27
subsistence, basic right to, 3, 4, 5, 6–11, 13–18, 26, 65–77, 81, 82, 87, 89, 94n5, 101, 104, 105, 106, 107, 109n7, 111, 113; arguments for, 66–67; critique of, 74–75, 103; definition of, 66, 69, 77n1; as limitation to property rights, 6–7, 14, 16, 65, 68–70, 77n6; as manifesto right, 13, 74
suum, 35–36, 38, 47, 48, 57, 58, 67
state of nature, 15, 77. *See also* Grotius, Hugo; Hobbes, Thomas; Pufendorf, Samuel
Stoicism, 38

Swanson, Scott G., 56–57, 58
sweatshops, 92, 96n27
Swedish Provincial Laws, 30
sympathy, 101

theft, 14, 21n49, 27, 29–30, 33, 42n34, 47, 49, 50, 51, 53, 99; petty, 10, 86, 112
Thomson, Judith Jarvis, 4, 85
Tierney, Brian, 31
Turkey, 112

Underland, 71, 89, 106
unfairness objection, 18, 87, 90–91, 99, 102, 108
Unger, Peter, 12–13; simple appropriation, 11–12
Universal Declaration of Human Rights, 77n1

urban homeless, 10, 14, 21n49, 82, 87–88, 94n14, 97. *See also* squatters

Van Duffel, Siegfried, 42n28
violence, 87, 88, 105, 107

Waldron, Jeremy, 6
war cosmopolitanism. *See* cosmopolitanism
water, 1, 47, 49, 66, 81, 82; wars, 88
wealth inequality, 1, 9, 20n29
welfare state, 49
Why Me? objection, 101–104

Yap, Dennis, 42n28
Young, Iris Marion, 9, 83, 110n19